BURMA AND JAPAN SINCE 1940

BURMA AND JAPAN SINCE 1940

From 'Co-prosperity' to 'Quiet Dialogue'

BY DONALD M. SEEKINS

NIAS Monograph 106

First published in 2007
by NIAS Press
NIAS – Nordic Institute of Asian Studies
Leifsgade 33, DK-2300 Copenhagen S, Denmark
tel: (+45) 3532 9501 • fax: (+45) 3532 9549
email: books@nias.ku.dk • website: www.niaspress.dk

Typeset by Thor Publishing
Produced by SRM Production Services Sdn Bhd
and printed in Malaysia

British Library Cataloguing in Publication Data
Seekins, Donald M.
  Burma and Japan since 1940 : from 'co-prosperity' to 'quiet
  dialogue'. - (NIAS monographs ; 106)
  1.Burma - Foreign relations - Japan 2.Japan - Foreign
  relations - Burma 3.Japan - Foreign relations - 1945-
  4.Burma - Foreign relations - 1948-
  I.Title
  327.5'91052

          ISBN-10: 87-91114-98-5
          ISBN-13: 978-87-91114-98-4

CONTENTS

FIGURES

TABLES

PREFACE

Keng Tung, one of the old Shan States located in eastern Burma, claims one of the earliest historical connections with Japan. The people of Keng Tung, the *Tai Khun*, believe that their traditional dress and hairstyle were inspired by Japanese styles. According to legend, in the sixteenth or seventeenth centuries a band of samurai, shipwrecked on the coast of Siam, were captured by the King of Siam and sent to Chiang Mai, in what is now northern Thailand. From there, they went to Keng Tung and intermarried with the local nobility. In Mi Mi Khaing's words, 'Whether this tale be fact or legend, it is still possible for the imaginative to read in the features of certain members of the ruling family and other official *Khun* families a Japanese cast.'[1]

Some centuries later, the Kinwun Mingyi, Burma's premier statesman under King Mindon (r. 1853–1878), had the good fortune to meet a Japanese gentleman at a party given by the Prince of Wales during his diplomatic visit to London in 1872. His words, reprinted in *Burma*, a journal published by the pro-Japanese government of Dr. Ba Maw in 1944, are worth quoting in full:

> I met a Nipponese [*sic*] who had been sent by the Emperor of Nippon to stay (in England) for his education and for the study of manners and customs (of the English people). He was dressed in European fashion and in the course of conversation, he told me that in Nippon, the construction of factories, mills, railways was going on apace. He further informed me that State Scholars (from his country) both male and female had been sent to America, England, France, Italy, Russia, Prussia, Austria, etc., and that the number of such scholars sent by the Emperor of Nippon was

over six hundred. He then added that Nippon was an Oriental country in the same way as Burma, and pointed out the possible benefits that would accrue by these two countries having mutual intercourse. He was very friendly toward me and expressed the hope that a closer, cordial, and happy relationship would be maintained between the two countries ... [2]

Such a relationship was not to be, because Britain extinguished Burma's independence just thirteen years later, in 1885. Between that year and 1941, the Japanese presence in Burma was largely commercial. But in the early years of the twentieth century, Japan's victory over Russia in the 1904–1905 war impressed many Burmese, as it did other Asians.[3] U Ottama, a Buddhist monk who was a pivotal figure in Burma's first stirrings of nationalism, lived in Tokyo, a teacher of Pali, the language of the Theravada Buddhist scriptures. But U Ottama's political inspiration came not from the east but from the west: Mahatma Gandhi and his *satyagraha* (truth struggle) movement in India. It was not until the eve of the Pacific War that Japan began to play a major role in Burma's history, through its support of young Burmese student nationalists led by Aung San.

This monograph is a discussion of Burma–Japan ties during three distinct periods: (1) the war and Japanese occupation of 1941–1945, when Burma was part of the 'Greater East Asia Co-Prosperity Sphere', an experience which had a formative impact on the country's subsequent development; (2) the 1954–1988 period, when ties between Tokyo and Rangoon were chiefly economic, and Japanese official development assistance (ODA) played a major role in the country's economy; and (3) the period after 1988, when the Japanese government sought, chiefly through economic inducements, to promote political and economic liberalization and to counteract the growing influence of the People's Republic of China. Over the years, Japanese have tended to view Burma through the veil of sentimentality ('the friendliest country in Asia toward Japan' because of wartime ties and imagined cultural affinities) while keeping a sharp eye on the bottom line (resource-rich Burma's role in Tokyo's strategies of economic survival).

Burma's leaders have alternately viewed Japan as an opportunity and a threat.

My research on Burma–Japan relations began in the early 1990s, and has been presented in articles in *Asian Survey*, *The Journal of Burma Studies* and *Burma Debate*, in a *Working Paper* published by the Japan Policy Research Institute, and in a conference paper given at the First Conference of the Swedish Association of Asia–Pacific Studies in Gothenburg in 2002 (see Bibliography and References). This book represents an expansion and updating of that research to the opening years of the new century. I was initially quite critical of what appeared to be Japan's indecisive and ambiguous approach to the post-1988 political crisis, stressing the continued dominance of business interests within the Japanese political system. But Burma–Japan relations, especially after 1988, have to be seen within a wider context: the failure of the international community to respond imaginatively and flexibly to the Burmese political crisis. Neither Tokyo's policy of 'quiet dialogue' (the use of behind the scenes or person-to-person diplomacy and economic inducements to encourage reform) nor the more critical, sanctions-oriented policies of the United States and other western countries has succeeded in influencing the behaviour of the ruling junta. Backed by China and to a lesser extent by fellow members of the Association of South East Asian Nations, the State Peace and Development Council eschews reconciliation with the pro-democracy opposition and continues to shape policies in conformity with its overriding agenda: protecting its political and economic monopoly. Under these circumstances, it is very difficult to be optimistic about Burma's future.

Okinawa, April 2006

NOTES

[1] Mi Mi Khaing (1960).

[2] *Burma* (1944: 43).

[3] Furnivall (1948: 143).

ACKNOWLEDGEMENTS

I would like to express my appreciation to Professor Vincent K. Pollard of the University of Hawaii for having made useful comments on this book when it was in the manuscript stage, and to the publishing firm Ōtō Shobō in Tokyo for having granted me permission to reproduce Figure 2 (p. 109) from their *manga* on the life of Aung San Suu Kyi. Many persons, including diplomats and people living inside of Burma, have provided me with information on the complexities of Burma–Japan relations and how they have changed over the years. The confidentiality of their comments must be protected, but I am most grateful for their insights. Finally, I wish to thank my wife Reiko for composing English translations of Japanese sources quoted in the book.

Chapter One

BURMA IN WORLD WAR II

THE PARADOXES OF STATE- AND ARMY-BUILDING

According to a brief section titled 'Dai Tōa Kaigi to Ajia Shokoku' (The Greater East Asia Conference and the Countries of Asia) in the controversial *Atarashii Rekishi Kyōkasho* [*New History Textbook*] approved by Japan's Ministry of Education in 2001:

> Among Japan's leaders, there were many who thought it necessary to strengthen military control of the occupied areas in order to carry out the war effort. However, in order to satisfy the expectations of people in these territories, Japan granted independence to Burma and the Philippines in 1943 (Shōwa 18), and extended formal recognition to the Provisional Government of Free India.
> Moreover, Japan, in order to gain their greater cooperation in the war, convened a Greater East Asia Conference in November 1943 in Tokyo with representatives from each of the territories. Major themes of the Conference were the sovereignty, independence, and cooperatively beneficial economic development of each nation, and the abolition of racial discrimination, as expressed in the Greater East Asia Proclamation. This embodied the ideals of Japan's war effort and was meant as a response to the Atlantic Charter promulgated by the Allied Nations [in 1941].[1]

The section concludes by mentioning the role of the Japanese-sponsored Indian National Army in that country's struggle for independence from Britain, achieved in 1947, and Burma's success in breaking free of British rule the following year. 'In these areas [i.e., South and Southeast Asia], movements for independence intensified, compared to the pre-war period, and so it can be said that the Japanese military's advance into the southern regions (*Nippon gun no Nampō shinshutsu*) speeded up the independence of Asian countries [from colonial domination].'[2]

The language of the *New History Textbook* is concise and muted. But academic Hasegawa Michiko asserts an unequivocal 'affirmation' of Japan's war and its accomplishments in a 1983 *Chūō Kōron* article:

> Did our Greater East Asia War really result in total defeat? The former colonies that all became battlegrounds all gained their independence during or after the war, and they have not fallen into white hands again. What are we to make of this fact? In the postwar years we were taught that this was an incidental byproduct of that detestable war. Yet as Japan's official statements on war objectives make clear, the goal was to free Asia from British and American domination and establish the area's self-defense and independence. Again, if one asks Japanese war veterans why they fought, the reply comes that they believed they were fighting to liberate Asia. And indeed, Asia was liberated. It is a curious logic that denies any connection between this purpose and the war's outcome. Is history so difficult that it can only be understood through such a strange logic?[3]

Drawing on the earlier work of Hayashi Fusao (*Dai Tōa Senso Kōteiron* [*Affirmation of the Greater East Asia War*]), Hasegawa defines what other writers have called the Fifteen Years' War (1931–1945) as the culmination of a '100 years' war' which began when the western powers invaded East Asia in the mid-nineteenth century.[4] Moreover, the 'Greater East Asia War' was not fought in Japan's national interest but to defend Asia's cultural integrity (its 'cultural sphere') and very existence, which was being 'choked' by the aggressive westerners. That Japanese soldiers wound up fighting Asians was regrettable, even tragic, Hasegawa admits (one is reminded of what the American military used to say in Vietnam, that 'we had to destroy that village in order to save it'). But it was a war with a higher purpose than mere empire-building.[5]

These two passages present us with two rather different propositions: first, that the Japanese 'advance' into Southeast Asia speeded up the process of decolonization, though it is not argued in the *New History Textbook* that if the 'Greater East Asia War' had not occurred, the European colonies of Southeast Asia would *never* have achieved independence; secondly, and far more ambitiously (here I refer to Hasegawa's passage), that the essence of the war was a survival struggle of Asian peoples against the West, and that this war was *successful* (thus, worthy of affirmation) since it resulted in the fall of the European colonial empires. Hasegawa compares the war-as-decolonization with Lincoln's emancipation of the slaves during the Civil War. Cynically, it seems, for she comments that Lincoln is given credit for freeing the slaves because he won his war, while the Japanese accomplishment ('an incidental byproduct of that detestable war') is belittled because Japan lost.[6]

A closer look at the historical sources shows that the Japanese occupation of Southeast Asia is difficult to define simply in terms of 'affirmation' or denial. In talking about 'colonialism' or 'the colonies', we often overlook the fact that each country in Southeast Asia, and each of the British, Dutch, French, and American colonial regimes that governed them, was different. The Japanese impact on each of them, and on different peoples inside each country, also varied remarkably, so that we can speak of the Chinese in Singapore and Malaya enduring systematic atrocities during 1942–1945 – the Japanese-instigated *sook ching* extermination campaign, which claimed thousands of victims among Chinese males – while the indigenous Malays' rural way of life was minimally affected, apart from Tokyo's sporadic policy of promoting Emperor worship among devout Muslims.[7]

Indeed, if any generalization can be made about the 'Greater East Asia War', it is that it *tore apart* societies – ethnically, religiously, and in terms of social class – that had already been weakened by the contradictions of colonial rule and economic globalization. Some nations have been able to overcome this fragmentation in the decades since the war (Malaysia and Singapore, for example).

Others have not (principally Burma), and arguably continue to suffer because of the legacies of the war.

Burma (known officially since 1989 as Myanmar) is the most interesting case study of the 'Greater East Asia War' and its impact. This is true for three reasons. First, Japanese revisionists often hold up Burma as the prime example of the liberating agenda of the war, since most of the country's post-independence leaders (Aung San, U Nu, Ne Win) came to prominence under Japanese auspices in 1941–1945. Secondly, the Japanese established what became independent Burma's most important political, economic and (with the possible exception of the Buddhist monkhood) social institution, the *Tatmadaw*, or armed forces. Burma has been governed as an 'Army-State' since March of 1962. Thirdly, Burma's 'Japanese interlude' represented a fundamental turning point in its development, more significant than achievement of formal independence in 1948 and arguably as significant as its colonization by the British in the nineteenth century. Different parts of Burma have been battle zones since the first Japanese forces crossed over from Thailand in the opening weeks of the war. The ongoing civil war has turned what was once a prosperous and cosmopolitan country into one of Asia's poorest and most isolated. Looking more closely at the Burmese case, we can see why the revisionist 'affirmation' of the war is problematic, to say the least.

BRITISH BURMA: DYNAMIC, BUT DIVIDED

What follows is a fairly detailed description of Burma under British rule just before the outbreak of the war, since I believe no assessment of the Japanese interlude is complete without considering what went before. If one assumes that the colonial regime was totally bad, and moreover incapable of reforming itself, then its overthrow in 1941–1942 must be a welcome thing, analogous to the Vietnamese invasion of Cambodia in 1978–1979, which got rid of the Pol Pot regime. But if one takes another position, that the colonial system, seriously flawed though it was, was capable of evolving into a post-colonial situation on its own, *peacefully*, then the Japanese 'liberation' of Burma looks like something quite different.

In the years leading up to the Pacific War, Burma was Southeast Asia's most developed country. It was blessed with rich natural resources, including abundant land for the cultivation of rice (between the late 19th century and the war, Burma was the world's largest exporter of rice to world markets), teak (with forests protected by strict conservation measures), petroleum, rubber, tin, tungsten, lead, silver, jade (mostly exported to China, where it is still highly prized), and the world-famous 'pigeon blood' rubies. Except for poor Indian labourers and the more primitive upland ethnic groups, whom the British called 'hill tribes', standards of living for just about everyone were higher than in most other parts of Asia due to the abundance of food and other necessities, though the economic position of ordinary Burmese farmers had deteriorated by the late 1930s, for reasons to be discussed below. Rangoon (population in 1931: 400,000) rivalled Shanghai and Tokyo as one of Asia's most modern and cosmopolitan cities, though its prosperity was based on exports of raw materials rather than manufacturing.

Colonial Burma had a well developed civil society, centred on Rangoon, embracing diverse religious, occupational, ethnic and political associations, print media which were largely, though not completely, free to criticize the government, and a high quality University of Rangoon which nurtured a new generation of intellectual and political leaders. That the university and the élite secondary schools taught in English gave educated Burmese a facility in the language rivalled only in India.

During times of popular unrest or insurgency, such as the 1930–1931 Saya San rebellion, the heavily-armed British colonial government crushed its armed opponents with brute force. But the rule of law was firmly established, and the Burmese, who have their own sophisticated legal traditions, became such eager litigants under British rule that a retired executive of the Irrawaddy Flotilla Company comments that his firm earned a large percentage of its profits from conveying people back and forth to the courts in Lower

Burma.[8] The political system was not genuinely democratic, since the British governor had authority independent of the legislature in the constitutional system established in 1935. Mostly British but with a handful of Burmese, the élite civil servants had powers comparable to Japan's present-day *kanryō* (élite bureaucrats). But Burmese who wished to make use of them had freedoms that people in French Indochina or the Netherlands East Indies could only dream about.[9]

Burmese high school and university students were a prominent and much admired group in colonial society, and their rather playful political activism during the late 1930s resembled that of American and European students in the 1960s rather than Burmese oppositionists today, who face jail, torture, possibly death. By the late 1930s, the two most important political groups were the Rangoon University Students' Union (RUSU), which became radicalised under the leadership of Aung San (the father of the present-day opposition leader Aung San Suu Kyi) and Thakin Nu (later U Nu, Burma's first prime minister after independence), and the Thakin Party, or Dobama Asiayone ('We Burmans Association'), established in 1930 by young urban intellectuals.[10] The Thakins, who by the end of the decade included the student leaders Aung San and Nu, led the drive for independence and attacked mainstream politicians for being subservient to the colonial overlords.

Their worldview, hardly a coherent ideology, was a lively blend of diverse trends: politicised Buddhism, Indian nationalist ideas, Irish Sinn Feinism, fascism, non-revolutionary Fabian socialism, and Sun Yat-sen's *San Min Chu-i*. The principal influence, however, was Marxism–Leninism. Thakin Nu established the *Nagani* or 'Red Dragon' Book Club in 1937. Many of its publications were Marxist literature, translated into Burmese from western languages.[11] All the most important young nationalists, including Aung San and Thakin Nu, were leftists. In 1939, they established the Communist Party of Burma, though Aung San, the party secretary-general, seems never to have been a committed communist.

Outwardly prosperous, Burma's society under colonial rule suffered from serious contradictions. Most Burmese living in the central part of the country – especially the Burmans, the ethnic majority who compose around 60–66 per cent of the population – did not regard British rule as legitimate. The older generation looked with nostalgia back on the Konbaung Dynasty, which the British abolished in 1885 at the end of the Third Anglo–Burmese War. They also feared that under alien rule the Buddhist religion, which had always been generously supported by the old kings, would perish amidst the flood of foreign influences, including missionary Christianity. The younger generation, informed by leftist ideology, sought a radical new synthesis of Buddhism, socialism and nationalism that would restore the country's independence and cure its social and economic ills.

Most ordinary Burmese found the elaborate 'self-government' apparatus established by the British on the local and national levels simply irrelevant, and declined to participate in elections and other aspects of public life. According to John S. Furnivall, a perceptive observer of the colonial regime, 'Self-government was impossible because there was no self to govern itself.'[12] By 'self', he meant a citizenry sharing common values, an appreciation of the public interest.

Furnivall called this phenomenon of public disengagement the 'plural society', symptomatic of colonial 'tropical economies'. What it meant was not simply that different cultural groups, with their own distinct values and customs, lived adjacent to each other (but not together) under a common authority, but that these groups, struggling to survive in an economically rational environment ('buy cheap, sell dear'), had nothing in common, lived in a state of mutual suspicion and anomie, and indeed were often at each others' throats. For example, there were race riots between Burmese and Indians in Rangoon in 1930 and 1938, in which hundreds of Indians were killed. As is true in today's globalised economy – indeed, the colonial plural society is a cautionary tale for twenty-first century globalisers – different groups were unequally prepared in terms of cultural values, levels of skill, political connections, and material wealth to compete in the modern economy, and there were clearly recognizable ethnic winners and losers. This competition became politicised (thus, the radicalism of the young nationalists), especially as world economic conditions after 1929 made the suffering of the losers even worse.

Immigrants, mostly Hindu and Muslim Indians with smaller numbers of Chinese and Europeans, sought economic opportunities. The immigration of Indians was facilitated by the fact that, until the Government of Burma Act was implemented in 1937, Burma was a province of the British Indian Empire and restrictions on their movements could not be imposed. By 1931, over fifty per cent of Rangoon's residents were from the subcontinent (only 35 per cent were Burmese), and Indians (including people from what are now Pakistan and Bangladesh) formed seven per cent of the entire country's population, or more than one million people.[13] Most Indians were concentrated in urban areas, and in Lower (southern) Burma.

The colonial regime's economic policy was *laissez faire*, combining limited public investment in infrastructure (railroads, inland waterways) with a business-friendly legal regime. Foreigners, including not only British and other European owners of large corporations such as the Irrawaddy Flotilla and Burmah Oil but also Indian and Chinese entrepreneurs, dominated the modern, export-oriented economy, and local economies as well. Burmese farmers benefited from the boom in rice exports in the late nineteenth century, but by the early twentieth century were squeezed by low prices (often artificially low, due to collusion by buyers even when world prices were high), indebtedness, and forfeiture of their family farms to moneylenders, many of whom were members of the much-disliked South Indian Chettiar caste. The Chettiars became absentee landlords, whose large estates formed over a quarter of Lower Burma's agriculturally rich lands by 1937.[14] Dispossessed Burmese farmers became their tenants, or joined the growing ranks of the unemployed who drifted into the cities and competed with low paid Indians for scarce jobs.

Indians worked as urban and rural labourers, often under conditions of extreme poverty, but they also filled the lower ranks of the civil service (fifty per cent of all government employees were Indian), the professions (including most physicians), and (along with Karens and other indigenous ethnic minorities) the police and colonial army. A majority of office workers in the big corporations were Indians, as were many merchants, shopkeepers, and craftsmen. Many members of the much smaller Chinese community excelled in business, like their counterparts in Malaya and Singapore, though the Burmese resented them less than they did the Indians because they assimilated more easily into Burmese society; indeed, many prominent members of Burmese society, including the late dictator Ne Win, were Sino-Burmese. Although there were some Burmese capitalists, a handful of moneylenders and rice millers, they were the exception rather than the rule.

A second major division in colonial Burma, one which had a still greater impact on the country's subsequent development than the plural society, was between the lowland, rice-cultivating peoples of central Burma (what the British called 'Burma Proper'), and the so-called 'hill tribes' who lived along the country's borders with China, Thailand, French Indochina and India. More than forty per cent of Burma's land area but a much smaller percentage of its population were included in the 'Frontier Areas', which were administratively separate from Burma Proper, and where local rulers enjoyed considerable autonomy. The Frontier Area contained a diverse array of groups including the Shans, a sophisticated people whose princes governed thirty-three semi-independent states in eastern Burma (present-day Shan State), the Karens, who also lived in large numbers in the Irrawaddy Delta south of Rangoon, the Karenni, Kachins, Chins, Nagas, and Wa (the latter with an unsavoury reputation as headhunters). Altogether, there are about forty to fifty major minority groups.

With the principal exception of the Shans, most of the Frontier Area peoples were originally not Buddhists but animists. In the nineteenth century, western missionaries converted many to Christianity, and graduates of mission schools became the new élites of the Karen, Kachin and Chin communities. Although Christians formed only a minority of Karens (most were, and are, animists and Buddhists), they were especially determined to assert the identity of their people, and with British encouragement established the Karen National Association in 1881, one of Burma's earliest political associations. Karen and Burman/Burmese nationalism were quite separate developments, often at odds with each other during the twentieth century.

Bonds between the 'hill tribes' and the British were strong. The British trusted the upland ethnic groups more than the Burmans, and encouraged their enlistment in the colonial army and police. During the Third Anglo–Burmese War (1885) and the 'pacification' that followed it (1885–1890), Karens and other minority soldiers fought alongside the British against Burman insurgents. In 1941–1945, they also fought together against the Japanese.

'Divide and rule' worked plenty of mischief, setting different groups against each other. At Rangoon University, stolid but hard-working Karen students were often regarded by their Burman classmates as 'pets' of their British teachers. When political activism became a student pastime during the 1930s, Christian Karens generally avoided it.

The division of Burma into two administratively distinct entities, Burma Proper and the Frontier Areas, meant that the country was never really united under a single government, though separate civil services in each region were under the authority of Burma's governor. Burma Proper had a semi-parliamentary system by the late 1930s, while the British preserved the 'feudal' character of chiefly or princely rule in the Frontier Areas. Unlike Burma Proper, the Frontier Areas were subjected to systematic neglect, due to chronically slim budgets. They had next to nothing in the way of social services such as public education and health (though missionaries often filled the gap), and were not developed economically save for jade mines in the Kachin hills and the Namtu lead and silver mine in the Shan States. Then as now, the two regions were remote from each other, their inhabitants living in largely different worlds, making national unity next to impossible.

Without attributing particularly benevolent motives to the British, who above all wanted Burma to turn a profit and, with a few exceptions, maintained a cool and distant attitude toward their native subjects, as amply illustrated by George Orwell in his novel *Burmese Days*, it is reasonable to suggest that British Burma was a work in progress. Given time and peaceful conditions, some of the problems connected with the plural society and the lack of integration between Burma Proper and the Frontier Areas could have been worked out. This is not to suggest that Burma should have remained British. By the late 1930s, most intelligent people in Britain and the colonies alike knew that the 'Age of Empire' was drawing to a close. This would have been true even if the 'Greater East Asia War' had not spread to Southeast Asia.

During the 1920s and 1930s, British colonialism in Burma, relatively liberal compared to the Dutch regime in Indonesia or the French in Indochina, was caught in an ultimately fatal contradiction. Outside of some indigenous and immigrant minority groups such as the Karens, the people regarded their British masters coolly, without enthusiasm. A vocal minority, with broad popular support, saw them as illegitimate. As mentioned, when open resistance such as the Saya San peasant revolt of 1930–1931 broke out, it was brutally suppressed.

But Britain had parliamentary government, and colonial policymakers could not ignore public opinion at home (though they listened less attentively to opinion in Burma itself, a major source of alienation). Burmese political demands – as opposed to armed insurgency – could not be dealt with by using bullets.

Wary of public opinion at home, insufficiently bloody-minded to crush unarmed civil dissent in the manner of the notorious General Dyer,[15] the colonial regime was in a quandary by the late 1930s. Plans for granting Burma Dominion status were discussed amongst British officials and the more conservative Burmese politicians, but no schedule for the achievement of self-rule within the British Commonwealth was announced. Massive demonstrations upcountry and in Rangoon in 1938–1939 won popular support for the radicals, especially the Thakin Party, which rejected any kind of cooperation with the colonial regime. After war broke out in Europe in September 1939, the Churchill government short-sightedly demanded that India and Burma contribute to Britain's defence without offering anything concrete in return. Churchill's determination to maintain the colonial status quo drove both established politicians such as Dr. Ba Maw and the militant Thakins into an alliance, and set the stage for Japanese intervention.

THE JAPANESE INTERLUDE

Burma during the war was like grass trampled by fighting elephants. Not only was it a major battlefield, involving hundreds of thousands of Allied and Japanese troops in pitched engagements up and down the country, but it was fought over twice: first, when the Japanese successfully drove the British out in 1942, capturing Rangoon in March and Mandalay in May; and secondly in 1944–1945 when British Commonwealth and other Allied forces commenced an offensive after the collapse of the disastrous Japanese Imphal Campaign, launched from Burma into north-eastern India. The Allies moved into northern Burma in late 1944–early 1945 and recaptured Rangoon by May 1945. According to D.G.E. Hall, 'Seen as a whole, the battle for Burma was the largest single action fought against the Japanese.'[16] Untold numbers of Burmese died, mostly from disease or starvation.

In general, Burmese (or Burmans) seemed to have welcomed the arrival of the Japanese, viewing them as liberators. But hospitable feelings were short-lived. Many Japanese troops had fought for years in China, and viewed local populations as enemies. Slapping the faces of civilians became routine. The *Kempeitai* (Japanese military police), ostensibly on the lookout for British spies and communists, conducted a reign of terror, detaining and torturing people for little or no reason. Its behaviour became so bad that wartime leader Ba Maw had to intercede with the highest military commanders to curb the worst excesses. Throughout the war, he found that the most difficult Japanese to handle were the 'Korea clique', officers who had picked up a deep racial arrogance in Japan's old colonies.[17]

In addition, Burmese were recruited for Ba Maw's 'Sweat Army', essentially forced labourers who worked under inhuman conditions, especially on the Thai–Burma Railway, the so-called

---

The Battles of Burma, 1941–42 and 1944–45

By the end of January 1942, the Japanese Fifteenth Army had captured Kawthaung, Burma's southernmost point, Tavoy, Mergui and Moulmein. Crossing the Sittang River in late February, it controlled Rangoon by 9 March. British forces, aided by Chinese Nationalist divisions based in Yunnan, hoped to hold Upper (northern) Burma, but the Japanese offensive moved swiftly north, capturing Mandalay on 1 May 1942 and Lashio, where the Burma Road began, on 8 May. British forces commanded by General William Slim staged a retreat into India under harsh conditions, but remained largely intact, ready to fight another day.

Japanese victory was assured by air superiority, and above all superior mobility and tactics, which enabled them to repeatedly outflank the British. However, they were not able to keep the advantage. The Allies perfected combined ground-air operations, as shown in the 'Chindit' operations of 1943 and 1944 commanded by General Orde Wingate, and 'Merrill's Marauders', an American force. The Imphal Campaign of March-June 1944 was a disaster for the Japanese, costing them tens of thousands of casualties and undermining their ability to defend Upper Burma. Slim began an offensive into northern Burma in late 1944, crossing the Irrawaddy in February 1945 and reoccupying Mandalay on 19 March. Thereafter, his forces steamrolled into Lower (southern) Burma, and Rangoon fell without a fight on 2–3 May.

The Japanese suffered over 185,000 deaths in Burma both in battle and due to disease and starvation. Many were killed by ethnic minority guerrillas, especially the Karens. British and Commonwealth forces suffered some 74,000 casualties, and the Chinese a much higher number, though uncounted. For the most complete account, see Louis Allen, *Burma: the Longest War* (London: Phoenix, 2000).

'railway of death'.[18] Deprived of food, shelter and medical treatment, tens of thousands died laying tracks through the fever-ridden, mountainous jungle. The post-1988 military regime has also used forced labour on a large scale, including for the construction of a rail line between Ye and Tavoy in southern Burma, which has been called a 'second railway of death'.

As Japanese forces advanced into the country in early 1942 and the situation looked increasingly hopeless, the British carried out a 'policy of denial', destroying much of Burma's excellent infrastructure, including rail lines, most of the river boats operated by the Irrawaddy Flotilla, oil refineries and communications networks. Japanese and British air raids wreaked havoc on Burma's cities. During the March 1945 battle for Mandalay, the beautiful royal palace built by King Mindon in the 19th century was burned to the ground.

It took more than a decade to repair the economic damage. Japan played an important role in reconstruction, signing a treaty with the government of independent Burma in 1954 to provide US$250 million in war reparations, supplemented in the 1960s by a further US$140 million in 'semi-reparations'.[19] But the easy prosperity of the pre-war years was a thing of the past.

The influx of arms during 1941–1945 and the creation of armed units in Burma Proper and the Frontier Areas, both national armies and local militias, made for an environment not unlike that of Afghanistan today. After foreign enemies were finished fighting the big battles, local warlords and ethnic minority rebels continued to settle scores and push their own agendas through the barrel of a gun. The resort to force became a reflex, and remained one long after 1945.

Both the colonial and wartime periods posed problems for the country's national identity, its 'state-ness', aptly symbolized by the 1945 destruction of Mindon's palace. The British colonial regime was not concerned with nation building. The political entity they governed was an assemblage of ethnic groups living under one or the other of two separate administrations, in Burma Proper and the Frontier Areas. British Burma, despite its economic dynamism, civil society, and high education standards, was a Rube Goldberg contraption, rife with internal contradictions, which collapsed easily under external pressure.

The Japanese impact on the country during 1941–1945 was to open up space within which a *Burman* nation could be constructed.

Both the Japanese and their collaborators – principally Dr. Ba Maw, who became head of the *Baho* or Central Executive Administration after the British were driven out in 1942 and in August 1943 *Nain-ngandaw Adipadi* or Head of State of 'independent' Burma within the Greater East Asia Co-Prosperity Sphere – were adept at symbolic politics, blending Pan-Asianism with evocations of Burma's pre-colonial glories. What Ba Maw calls the 'Burmese Era' was also a time of institution building under the auspices of the 'totalitarian' state that he established.[20] The most important institution, however, was the army, which was established not by himself but the Japanese, and which unlike its colonial counterpart was largely if not exclusively Burman.

In other words, radical political and social changes made possible during the Japanese occupation created a 'post-colonial' state with an evocative and authentic (though selectively constructed) national identity, *for the ethnic majority*. But this was achieved at the price of excluding most of the indigenous and foreign ethnic minorities from the political-military centre. And after 1941, the 'political' and 'military' spheres were inseparable, since men with guns, rather than colonial officials or elected politicians, dominated the political stage.

CHARACTERISTICS OF THE JAPANESE OCCUPATION

Until Burma became nominally independent in August 1943, it was governed by a Japanese Military Administration (*Gunseikanbu*), which viewed Burma primarily as a supplier of natural resources and manpower for the war effort. It was subordinate to the Southern Area Army, headquartered in Singapore, which had control over not only Burma but also large areas of Island Southeast Asia, and ultimately to Imperial General Headquarters (*Dai Hon'ei*) in Tokyo. Supreme executive authority was vested in the commander-in-chief of Japanese forces. The Imperial Army, independent of the Military Administration, wielded tremendous power.[21]

Most of the *Gunseikanbu* personnel were civilians employed by the Army, seconded from the Home Islands, who were responsible for securing the local population's cooperation through Ba Maw's 'Burma *Baho* [Central] Government'. On the regional and local levels, the administrative structure established by the British was largely preserved, and many British-era Burmese civil servants remained at their posts. Given the dislocations of the war, language barriers, and especially the divergent points of view held not only between Burmese and Japanese but also among the Japanese themselves (especially civilians versus Army officers), the system was not very efficient.

By the end of the war, Burmese civil servants in the districts and towns, who before 1941 were among the most respected people in the colonial society, had suffered a great fall in prestige, since they had been deprived of signs of high status by the wartime government – including the colonial-era expectation that ordinary people would prostrate before them, and call them *paya*, 'lord' – and were perceived as unable to shield the people from economic hardship or Japanese oppression.[22]

Although the *Gunseikanbu* was abolished after 'independence', Ba Maw's government, despite great efforts on his part, was unable to operate independently of the Japanese Commander-in-Chief. This meant that Ba Maw was widely dismissed as a Japanese puppet, the ruler of a monsoon 'Manchukuo' (the state established by the Japanese in northeastern China in 1932), who had no choice but to collaborate in the increasingly desperate Japanese expropriations as the end of the war drew near. In the economic sphere, the Japanese Army established a cartel arrangement of favoured companies who controlled manufacturing and the diminishing export-import trade. Because of Tokyo's policy of self-sufficiency in the occupied territories, which was made further necessary by the depredations of Allied submarines, the large number of Japanese soldiers (some 300,000) essentially lived off the land.[23]

Although Burma did not suffer the terrible famines of Japanese-occupied Java or northern Vietnam (or for that matter, Bengal in British-ruled India), the failure of Ba Maw and his elite civil servants to prevent falling standards of living and Japanese abuses of power, especially by the *Kempeitai*, resulted in their political sidelining after the war.[24] It was the Thakins, especially Aung San, whose originally collaborationist army at the beginning of the war had risen against the Japanese in March of 1945, who were able to lead the vanguard in the struggle for independence against a restored British regime.

BUILDING A BURMAN ARMY

From the beginning of their recorded history, the Burmans have cherished martial values, not unlike the Japanese. At its most powerful in the sixteenth and eighteenth centuries, the Burman state subjugated non-Burman states on the periphery of the Burman heartland (the Mons, Shans, Arakanese) and expanded into what are now Laos, Thailand and northeastern India. An eighteenth century Burmese king, Hsinbyushin, even defeated repeated Chinese invasions of the Shan States. The British colonial era, then, was something of a hiatus in which the Burmans were disarmed. The colonial armed forces consisted of soldiers brought over from India, or, as mentioned, non-Burman ethnic minorities. In 1939, the Burma Defence Force had in its ranks only 472 Burmans (a category which apparently also included Mons and Shans), compared to 3,197 Karens, Kachins and Chins.[25]

Rangoon University had a Training Corps that was popular with Burman students, though there was no opportunity for them to pursue a military career after graduation. The major political parties, including the Dobama Asiayone (Thakins), the Myochit or Patriot Party and even the Rangoon University Student Union, had paramilitary units (*tat* in Burmese) who guarded leaders, kept order during rallies, and sometimes acted like Mussolini's Blackshirts. Rejecting Mahatma Gandhi's non-violent methods of struggle, the Thakins employed militant, aggressive rhetoric and planned armed struggle against the colonial regime. The decision of the Imperial General Headquarters in late 1941 to give

Colonel Suzuki Keiji authority to organize a Burman armed force to assist in the Japanese invasion of the country had an immense psychological impact on the ethnic majority.

The establishment of the wartime army constitutes mythic history, involving the heroic adventures of Aung San and the 'Thirty Comrades'. Soon after the outbreak of war in Europe, Dr. Ba Maw, who had been ousted as prime minister following the anti-British demonstrations of 1938–1939, talked with the Japanese consul in Rangoon, sounding him out on getting financial and other assistance from Tokyo. One of his closest associates, Dr. Thein Maung, became head of the Japan–Burma Society after his visit to Tokyo in October–November 1939 (the Society's secretary was Colonel Suzuki).[26] As ties between Ba Maw, Aung San, and the Japanese grew closer, Tokyo loomed large in their planning for an anti-British underground movement. By this time Ba Maw and the Thakins had joined in a united front, the Freedom Bloc, and Aung San was the Bloc's secretary.

With a price set on his head by the British authorities, Aung San left Burma with a fellow Thakin in August 1940, bound for Amoy (Xiamen) on the China coast. Just whom he planned to contact remains unclear. In her biography of her father, Aung San Suu Kyi claims that his intention was to get support not from the Japanese but from the Chinese communists. When he and his comrade failed to contact communist agents, they reluctantly accepted the invitation of a Japanese agent to be flown to Tokyo to meet Colonel Suzuki.[27] In *The Minami Organ*, Izumiya Tatsurō, a wartime subordinate of Colonel Suzuki, cites a Burmese source that '(a)t Amoy, Aung San intended to make his way overland to Chungking [Chongqing] despite the length of the journey. But they did not succeed, and after wandering around aimlessly for a few months, [they] were contacted by one Major Kanda of the Japanese Military Police.'[28] In 'Burma's Challenge', Aung San indicates the mutual reluctance of the Japanese and leftists like himself ('Bolsheviks' in Japanese eyes) to cooperate, and that

I was sent out to China and given a blank cheque by my comrades to do what I thought best for my country. As the China–Burma Road was closed, I had to go to China by sea and that, even though insignificant in itself, caused our later association with the Japanese. I couldn't reach the interior of China [where the communists were based] by sea. I was told I could reach Amoy only and then would have to rely upon my own resourcefulness to get to the interior of China.[29]

Ba Maw's version of events written up in *Breakthrough in Burma* does not mention China, claiming that he, Aung San, Dr. Thein Maung and a Japanese diplomat planned Aung San's escape, and that Amoy was chosen as his destination since it was close to the Japanese colony of Taiwan. Though they arrived in Amoy without incident, the two Thakins spent a couple of desperate months, ill and short of funds, before Aung San wrote a letter to his comrades in Rangoon asking for help. Thein Maung arranged with 'Minami Masuyo' (Colonel Suzuki's assumed name, as he was then in Rangoon posing as a correspondent for the *Yomiuri Shimbun*) to have Taiwan-based *Kempeitai* agents rescue them.[30] There is no evidence that the two Thakins attempted to leave the port city and strike out for the interior.

In November 1940, they met Colonel Suzuki in Tokyo, where, Aung San comments, 'I had to make the best of a bad job'.[31] They agreed that Aung San would go back to Burma under cover to recruit more young men from his party to form the nucleus of an anti-colonial army. Though unenthusiastic about Japanese plans to invade Burma, he believed, rather naively, that while Japanese and British forces were fighting along the border, his new army could declare independence and seize power. Suzuki established a secret organization, the *Minami Kikan* (Minami Organ, *minami* being both Suzuki's cover name in Rangoon and the Japanese word for 'south'), to coordinate their activities in Thailand and other parts of Southeast Asia.

By summer 1941, 27 men from the Thakin Party had been smuggled out of Burma by sea and overland, and brought to Japan. Together with Aung San, his original Amoy companion and a Burmese student in Tokyo, they were taken to a specially constructed training facility at Sanya on the Japanese-occupied island of Hainan, China, to receive military instruction.[32] These men were the legendary Thirty Comrades, the core of the first Burman armed force since the fall of the Burman kingdom in 1885, the Burma Independence Army. Their training, which was so tough that at times some of the Thakins were on the verge of revolt, lasted from April until October.

The Japanese divided the Thirty Comrades into three groups: one group, including Aung San, were to assume command and administrative positions in the new army; a second group, including a Sino-Burmese Rangoon University dropout, Thakin Shu Maung (better known as Ne Win), were to carry out guerrilla and sabotage activities behind enemy lines; while the third group, composed of younger Thakins, received training as field commanders.[33] Because few if any of the trainees knew Japanese, instruction was carried out in broken English.

On both sides, the alliance was one of convenience. The Burmese needed foreign assistance. The Japanese, seeking a favourable end to their war with China, which had broken out in July 1937, wanted to shut down the Burma Road through which the Americans and British supplied Chiang Kai-shek at his wartime capital of Chongqing. After northern Vietnam fell into Japanese hands in September 1940, cutting off a rail route between Hanoi and China, the Burma Road, which wound through the mountains from the railhead at Lashio in Shan State to the Yunnan Province capital of Kunming, was Chiang's only outlet to the sea. According to Japanese sources, the volume of arms and supplies carried over the road expanded from 2,000 tons in 1939 to 10,000 tons in 1940.[34]

Following the Pearl Harbour attack and the landing of Japanese troops at Kota Baharu, Malaya, on 8 December 1941, the Thirty Comrades were brought to Bangkok, and on 28 December the Burma Independence Army (BIA) was officially established. Colonel Suzuki assumed command, while another Japanese officer was chief of staff. Aung San was designated senior staff officer, and Shu Maung appointed head of an army group in charge of 'interior sabotage'. Each of the Thirty Comrades took a *nom de guerre* reflecting pride in their new mission, including Aung San (Bo Teza, the 'fire commander') and Shu Maung (Bo Ne Win, the 'shining sun commander'). Suzuki assumed the name Bo Mogyo, 'commander thunderbolt', which showed his adroitness in manipulating cultural symbols. According to an old prophecy, Burma's British conquerors (symbolized by an umbrella) would be struck down by a thunderbolt. A rumour was let around that Suzuki was the descendant of Myingun Min, a prince of the defunct royal dynasty, thus a *minlaung* or pretender to the throne. On the day the BIA was founded, the Thirty Comrades performed the *thwe thauk* or blood drinking ceremony, in which each donated some of his blood, mixed with liquor, which they drank together. This ceremony, like the Bo Mogyo legend, drew deeply on Burma's warlike past.[35]

The BIA accompanied Japanese forces penetrating Burma in the first months of 1942. Its rank and file, which numbered as many as 30,000 (of whom only about 4,000 actually took part in military operations), was filled with Burmese living around Bangkok and the Thai–Burma border, augmented by thousands of young village volunteers inside Burma. Although the new army distinguished itself in several engagements with the British, notably at Shwedaung near Prome, a British intelligence report published in late 1943 says that '[a]bout half the BIA consisted of high minded young Nationalist idealists but the other half were mere thugs out for what they could make. Most of the members enlisted to get in on the ground floor of the new government.'[36] The BIA soon degenerated into an armed mob as law and order inside Burma broke down in the wake of the British retreat. This led to inter-ethnic violence that surprised even the Japanese (see 'Ethnic Conflict', p. 25).

Loved and feared by his men but an irritant to his superiors, 'Bo Mogyo' was relieved of his command, and sent home in June 1942. Ba Maw compared him to T.E. Lawrence, the agent of a big power who gains mastery of a small country's local knowledge, and seems to feel split loyalties. According to U Nu, Suzuki said that if the Japanese refused to grant Burma independence, 'Then tell them that you will cross over to some place like Twante [near Rangoon] and proclaim independence and set up your own government. If they start shooting, you just shoot back.'[37] This romanticism was at odds with the views of the top brass, who exercised tight control over the country in order to extract its natural resources.

With the establishment of the Burma Defence Army (BDA) in summer 1942, replacing the BIA, the rationalization of the armed forces was begun. The new army had a planned troop strength of 10,000 (British intelligence reports that only about 5,000 were actually mobilized by late 1943), and was a structured institution with a general staff and officers' and enlisted men's training facilities. In its first year of operation, the officers' training school at Mingaladon north of Rangoon trained 300 officers for the BDA, of whom the top 30 were sent to Japan for further training. During the war, a large number of Burman officers entered military academies in the Home Islands, absorbing Japanese military doctrine.[38]

By the time Burma was declared 'independent' by the Japanese in August 1943, the armed forces, renamed the Burma National Army (BNA) were free of formal Japanese control. According to U Maung Maung, there was little communication between the BNA at its headquarters in Rangoon and the Japanese command across town, except for liaison officers. Ne Win succeeded Aung San as commander-in-chief of the armed forces with the rank of colonel, while Aung San became defence minister in Ba Maw's cabinet.[39]

The impact of Japanese tutelage on the present *Tatmadaw* or armed forces is difficult to assess. Some of the Thirty Comrades were eager students. In U Maung Maung's words, 'They behaved and dressed as much like Japanese officers as they could.'[40] Others, including Ne Win, apparently resented the forceful imposition of Japanese values, especially during the time on Hainan. But Ne Win received counter-insurgency training from the *Kempeitai*, and the sophisticated Military Intelligence apparatus he established after Burma became independent may owe something to his Japanese teachers. After 1988, some democracy activists claimed the *Tatmadaw* copied its brutal pacification tactics in the Frontier Areas from the Japanese. There are more than superficial resemblances between the *Tatmadaw's* 'Four Cuts' policy against ethnic minority rebels (to cut, or deprive, rebels of recruits, funding, supplies and information) and the Japanese army's *sankō seisaku* or 'three all' policy in China ('kill all; burn all; destroy all').[41] But war atrocities have their own dynamic, and there is no reason to believe that an army largely unconstrained by public opinion or the rule of law – as Ne Win's was even before his coup d'état in 1962 – would have followed civilized rules of war, even if the Japanese had never come to Burma.

The most important of the Thirty Comrades and their Thakin comrades, many of whom had communist sympathies, had grown thoroughly disgusted with Japanese-style sham independence by mid-1944, and established an underground Anti-Fascist Organization with Aung San's blessing. As British Commonwealth forces fought their way into central Burma the following year, Aung San ordered the BNA to rise up against the Japanese on 27 March 1945. Allied with Louis Mountbatten's South-East Asia Command, they received a new designation, the Patriotic Burmese Forces (PBF). The twenty-seventh of March is now an important national holiday, originally known as (Anti-Fascist) Resistance Day but now Armed Forces Day. If the meaning of the original name celebrated the 'people's army's' determination to drive all foreign imperialists out of Burma, the later name highlighted the *Tatmadaw's* self-perception as the sole defender of the country's independence and sovereignty.[42]

In *Breakthrough in Burma*, Ba Maw writes that Aung San, despite his original misgivings about the Japanese, had by 1943 begun to absorb Japanese militarist values, asserting that the commander of the armed forces had the right to deal directly with the head of state, rather than through the cabinet. He also resented being called as a witness in a court case, saying that it was demeaning to the army. Ba Maw warned the young leader, 'Do not let such thoughts [Japanese victories in the war] make you too Japanese in the wrong things. Remember that the army belongs to the state, and not the state to the army.'[43] Aung San seems to have taken this lesson to heart, since after the war he frequently emphasized that the army must serve the people, rather than the other way around.[44] But he was assassinated by a political rival in July 1947. Burmese often call *Bogyoke* (General) Aung San the 'father of the Tatmadaw'. After his death, the army's 'stepfather', Ne Win, had rather different ideas.

In terms of personnel, the new Burma Army established by the British after their reoccupation of the country in 1945 was an unstable joining together of two antagonistic groups: BNA/PBF veterans, mostly Burmans, and ethnic minority 'class units' which had remained loyal to the Allies. A Karen, General Smith Dun, was appointed commander-in-chief. Ethnic minority soldiers outnumbered the Burman contingent, but the ethnic and communist revolts of 1948–1949 caused many minority troops to mutiny. Others were purged from the ranks. Smith Dun retired, to be replaced by Ne Win as supreme commander. From that time on, Ne Win and his close cronies from the wartime era dominated the military, and after 1962 the Army-State.

Ba Maw argues that Suzuki and Aung San's decision to recruit the Thirty Comrades from among a single faction of the Thakin Party rather than a plurality of factions aggravated the personalistic and factional nature of Burmese politics.[45] In fact, few of the Thirty Comrades had a role in the post-war state, especially the post-1962 Army-State. The most important legacy of Ne Win's rise to military prominence during the war was his establishment of a traditional Burmese-style personal dictatorship, centred on himself, in which he quite consciously assumed the role of king.

The Japanese did not build the Army-State that rules Burma today. But in promoting the rise of a Burman military largely independent of civilian authorities, much like their own, they planted seeds that grew during the ensuing post-war years of turmoil. The Japanese and their Burman allies succeeded in driving out the white colonialists, as Hasegawa has argued. But a worldview placing the military at the centre of the political system contributed to the establishing of a 'post-colonial' regime that, by the 1960s, was more oppressive than the colonial original. And as Lieutenant-General Khin Nyunt, former Prime Minister and head of Military Intelligence, once said: 'Our Tatmadaw was made in Japan.'[46]

ETHNIC CONFLICT

The central issue in Burmese politics today is not the well-publicized battle of wills between Daw Aung San Suu Kyi and the military junta, the State Peace and Development Council (SPDC), but how centuries of hostility between the ethnic minorities and the majority Burmans can be ended, how the different groups can be included in a new national community on the basis of equality. Minority scholars point to the fact that ethnic conflict, though not modern 'ethnic politics', has been going on since the beginning of the country's recorded history: for example, the Burman wars during the eleventh to eighteenth centuries against the Mons, who established sophisticated polities in Lower Burma. They argue that no political arrangement that ignores the aspirations of the minorities, especially in the Frontier or Border Areas, can bring genuine peace.[47]

The view espoused by the Burman military, especially since the establishment of the first Army-State by Ne Win in 1962, is diametrically opposed to this, asserting that although Burma is a multi-ethnic society, the different indigenous groups are fundamentally the same. According to one SPDC commentator, 'We all descended from the Mongolian Tribe and therefore we, the indigenous races, are not aliens but kith and kin.'[48] They claim that the present discord among ethnic groups is due to the colonial-era destruction of a primordial 'national identity'. The British policy of 'divide and rule', set 'kith and kin' against each other. The truth is that the British, determined to transform an unruly, independent kingdom into a pliable, money-making venture, made use of ethnic divisions, but did not invent them. Among the Karens, the old admonition of mothers to their children – 'Eat your rice quickly. The Burmans are coming!' – was not British propaganda, but part of their long history of oppression at Burman hands.

The Japanese interlude made the ethnic situation far worse than it was under British rule, for two reasons. First, the collapse of social order following their invasion set the different groups against each other, especially in Lower Burma. The level of violence was unprecedented. Secondly, the war put the minorities and the Burmans on different sides, the former largely supporting the British, the latter the Japanese – at least until the uprising of 27 March 1945.

After the British began their retreat from Burma in spring 1942, Karen soldiers serving in their ranks were discharged and went home to their villages, often bringing their arms with them. Because they refused to surrender their guns, they and their families soon became targets of the BIA, especially in the Irrawaddy Delta where a large number of Karens lived. Often, Karens joined forces with local Indians to fight the BIA and other Burmans. To punish Karen guerrillas for the death of one of his officers, Suzuki ordered the BIA to destroy two large Karen villages, killing all the men, women and children with swords. This incident ignited a race war, with more massacres on both sides, before the regular Japanese army could impose order and rein in the hooligan element in the BIA. The worst incidents were in the Myaungmya District south of Bassein in the Irrawaddy Delta, where an estimated 1,800 Karens were killed and 400 of their villages destroyed.[49]

According to Ba Maw, the Karens never forgot these incidents. One Karen leader told him that:

> As long as the Burmese [Burman] big race ways towards us do not change ... this rebellion, even if it should be crushed in the end by superior numbers and arms, will go on in the hearts of the Karens, and will break out again and again till the two races part for good.[50]

Most Karens and Karenni, a closely related people living along the Thai-Burma border, remained loyal to the British, carried out underground anti-Japanese operations, and received Allied arms shipments by air. In the last months of the war, Karen and Karenni guerrillas claimed to have killed 12,500 Japanese troops retreating to the Salween River.[51]

According to Ba Maw, ethnic violence in Arakan, western Burma, was even worse than that between Karens and Burmans.

Buddhist Arakanese and mostly Muslim Bengalis attacked each other, and Bengalis crossed over from what was still British territory to help their co-religionists.[52] Today, Karen guerrillas and Arakanese Muslim militants continue to resist the central government in two of the country's most tenacious insurgencies. In these areas of Burma, it is not incorrect to say that World War II continues.

During the opening months of the war, Burman nationalists 'solved' the plural society problem in a Gordian Knot manner. As the British began their retreat, Burman/Burmese mobs attacked Indians in urban and rural areas of Lower Burma, and hundreds of thousands of them left the country, often on foot through the densely jungled Arakan Yoma mountain range.[53] Tens of thousands died on the perilous journey back to their ancestral homelands, and of those who survived, few returned to Burma after the war. Although an Indian (or rather Indian, Pakistani, Bangladeshi) minority lives in Burma to this day, especially in Rangoon, the war marked the end of their prominent role in the country's multi-ethnic society.[54]

Of all the Frontier Area regions, the Shan States, a rich mosaic of diverse peoples, was the most fortunate. The Japanese prevented the BIA from entering the Shan States in 1942, probably in order to prevent more racial violence. The Shan *sawbwa* (princes) and other local rulers formally recognized Japanese rule. Although the easternmost principalities, Keng Tung and Mongpan, were handed over to Japan's ally, Thailand, the other Shan States became a part of 'independent' Burma in 1943. The rulers retained the autonomy they enjoyed under the British, and the region was spared the worst calamities of the war.

The situation was quite different in other parts of the Frontier Areas, where the Kachins, Chins and Nagas lived. Because the Japanese were unable to impose effective control over these peoples, who traditionally played an important part in the colonial armed forces, the British recruited them for underground operations and the major push against the Japanese in 1944–1945. Formerly remote and isolated, the Kachin districts (now Kachin

State) became a focal point of the Allied effort to recapture Burma. At one point, the airport located in the small town of Myitkyina (now Kachin State's capital) became the world's busiest as men and supplies were brought in for the campaign in Upper Burma.[55] More significantly, a generation of Kachin war veterans began their own resistance against the Rangoon government in the 1960s, establishing one of Burma's best-organized and effective guerrilla movements, the Kachin Independence Army.

Bitter wartime memories on the part of the minorities made post-war reconciliation almost impossible. Aung San, who had become Burma's most popular leader after the 27 March uprising, seems to have understood that national unity without free participation of the minorities was impossible. At the February 1947 Panglong Conference, he and minority leaders (with the prominent exception of the Karens) laid out the contours of a constitutional settlement establishing a quasi-federal structure of government. But as mentioned, Aung San was assassinated in July of that year. His successors, including even the sophisticated and democratically-inclined U Nu, were less sympathetic to the aspirations of the Frontier Area peoples.

The central government's Burman perspective, combined with the systematic 'Burmanisation' of the army in the late 1940s, combined to create a major national tragedy. By the mid-1980s, when Ne Win was still in power, the former Frontier Areas were dominated by a multi-hued array of ethnic, communist and drug-dealing armies, consisting of at least 28 major groups, of whom the largest, the People's Army of the Communist Party of Burma, commanded 15,000 men, mostly ethnic Wa. According to Martin Smith, this civil war cost an average of 10,000 military and civilian deaths a year between the 1950s and the late 1980s.[56] Though the overflow of the Chinese civil war into Shan State after 1949 and the heavy-handedness of post-1948 Burman governments were the major factors in the state's failure to achieve peaceful national unity, this war had its roots in the Japanese occupation.

BA MAW AND ASIAN 'IDENTITY'

The *Atarashii Rekishi Kyōkasho* mentions the Greater East Asia Conference of November 1943 as a focal point for Japan's vision for an Asia freed of Western colonialism. In *Breakthrough in Burma*, Ba Maw devotes a whole chapter to this event, claiming that it was the first expression of a new 'Asian' spirit, a sense of Asian unity and shared destiny, which found its post-war expression in the 1955 Bandung Conference of the Afro-Asian Nations and the Five Principles of Peaceful Coexistence, or Pancha Sila, which defined 'a new order in Asia'.[57]

It is easy to dismiss the Conference as nothing but empty words and gestures, especially since 'Greater East Asia' leaders who attended included Wang Ch'ing-wei, whose Nanking regime was propped up by Japanese bayonets, and the premier of Manchukuo, the original puppet state carved out of China by the Kwantung Army in 1931–1932.[58] But this propaganda had great appeal, even among Asians otherwise unenthusiastic about Japanese rule. In the words of the Joint Declaration issued at the end of the conference, the countries of 'Greater East Asia' will 'ensure the fraternity of nations in their region by respecting one another's independence and sovereignty'. This *ideological* contribution of the Japanese to 'Asian identity' was especially attractive to indigenous ethnic/religious majorities (Burmans, Malays, Javanese) who had been marginalized by the colonial plural society.

From the perspective of the beginning of the twenty-first century, the competing models of the western colonial order and the Asian regional unity proposed at the Greater East Asia Conference have an interesting resonance. British Burma was not democratic, but it was an economically liberal society in which different social groups could pursue their interests within the framework of law. It was, culturally, in terms of 'identity', a colourless entity, rational and driven by profit, much like the 'globalised' world order promoted today by the United States. It brought great prosperity, but also great inequality and injustice.

Because, as mentioned, the ethnic winners and losers were clearly identifiable, anti-colonial, nationalist movements such as the Thakins took on an intensely racial flavour, especially in regard to 'foreign' Asians such as the Indians. 'Race' was very much part of the 'Greater East Asia' worldview. In Ba Maw's speech at the Conference, he says, 'My Asiatic blood has always called to other Asiatics. In my dreams, both sleeping and waking, I have heard the voice of Asia calling to her children.'[59]

Ba Maw's state was *post-colonial* in the sense that, in principle at least, it promoted independence, sovereignty and an 'authentic' Burman culture. He was quite aware of Japanese motives in granting Burma 'independence' in 1943, but also saw the opportunities it presented for mobilizing the Burman population. Like Ne Win after 1962, the *Adipadi* borrowed the pomp of the old Burmese dynasties to promote national identity and his own legitimacy. He conducted himself, in manner and dress, like one of the old kings. He sponsored one public ceremony in which 'victory soil' was brought from Shwebo in Upper Burma, the town where Alaungpaya established the Konbaung Dynasty (1752–1885), and placed in a Rangoon park.[60] Thakin Kodaw Hmaing, Burma's greatest nationalist writer who drew deeply on the past to inspire the younger generation of Thakins, declared:

I have never been as happy during my long life as now. ...

It makes me happy beyond words to know that the British have been driven out of our country and a great Asian people have come to liberate another Asian people and given us back our ancient heritage, our land and freedom and religion and culture.[61]

The new Burman state was top-down and homogenizing. Its foundations were the 'leadership principle' ('the Japanese believed in the leadership principle and would only deal with us on that basis'), with Ba Maw himself designated *Adipadi* or Head of State in 1943; and the 'concept and technique of total organization in every area', including a single political party, the Dobama Sinyetha Asiayone (later known as the Maha Bama or Greater Burma

Party).[62] Ba Maw described the Maha Bama Party as 'a common melting pot for the native races of Burma from which will arise the Greater Burma nation. Our past tribal history has closed, tribal accounts are settled, and a new nation and history now begins. In the past, parties overshadowed peoples. Now we are unifying from the right end, from the people.'[63]

This statement points out the problematic nature of sovereignty and independence in the post-war Asian context. The post-colonial order has emphasized the singular autonomy of *the state* as the ultimate expression of *the nation's* ethnic, racial and cultural unity. What this means is that there is often little or no room for groups within society to assert their own autonomy, regardless of whether they are moderate or extreme, representing ethnic, religious or social interests. The intense preoccupation with unity and sovereignty expressed today by the Burmese military junta was anticipated by the paradoxical and privileged status given to these values at the Greater East Asia Conference. In other words, the Conference posed but did not answer the difficult question: 'independence' and 'sovereignty' *for whom*?

CONCLUSION: DID THE JAPANESE LIBERATE BURMA?

There is no doubt that the Japanese occupation hastened Burma's departure from the British Empire. Toward the end of the war, the Churchill government published a White Paper proposing that Burma Proper be returned to the pre-war, semi-parliamentary system after a few years of reconstruction, which was intended to benefit British business interests, with the ultimate goal of self-government. The Frontier Areas, however, would determine their own political future, either together or separate from Burma Proper. This was unacceptable to Aung San and his comrades, who wanted speedy independence and the immediate integration of the Frontier Areas with Burma Proper. Faced with the prospect of fighting a well-armed Burmese guerrilla army, Churchill's successor Clement Attlee gave in to Aung San's demands, and in January 1948 the new Union of Burma was born.

But war is a blunt instrument, and the old political and social order, imperfect as it was, could not be easily replaced. At the beginning of this chapter, I said that the Japanese occupation represented a fundamental turning point in the country's history, simply because after 1941, men with guns rather than politicians or colonial officials dominated the political stage. The war militarized Burma's society, and the impact of this can be seen six decades later in the political and economic *cul de sac* created by the State Peace and Development Council junta. Of course it is also true that Burma suffered the fate of being propelled directly from the Pacific War right into the Cold War, with the 1948 Communist Party of Burma uprising and large-scale Kuomintang incursions into Shan State in 1950.

One of the best sources on wartime Burma remains Dorothy Guyot's Ph.D. thesis, *The Political Impact of the Japanese Occupation of Burma*. She describes the impact of the Japanese interlude in terms of the realization of aspirations for independence, the sidelining of colonial era élites (including pre-war politicians and civil servants), the political mobilization of the masses, and perhaps most significantly, the 'glorification of violence during the war'.[64] The occupation made possible the emergence of a new modern élite, centred on the Thakins and others who participated in the anti-Japanese resistance. But the militarization and politicization of Burmese society did not create circumstances in which modern (or democratic) political institutions could flourish: even after the war, 'violence and destruction were forms of activity highly acceptable to young Burmese, and open to all who were so inclined. It was much more satisfying and less personally demanding than the humdrum chores mapped out by the élite for the reconstruction of society.'[65]

Guyot's thesis was completed in 1966, and from the perspective of the early twenty-first century we can see that the Burmese élite's antidote for anarchy and violence has been the imposition of an oppressive, homogenizing Army-State, itself a more terrible instrument of violence than the insurgent bands or ethnic minority insurgents who have roamed the countryside since the 1940s. Political development has not occurred, a constructive and non-coercive political order has not been achieved. In other words, the war and Japanese occupation laid the foundations for the establishment of an Army, and possibly a State (after 1962, an Army-State), but *not* a Nation.

The fundamental issue in nation-building is sovereignty. But sovereignty is not simply the replacement of white faces by brown ones at the apex of the state, the substitution of one ethnic-racial élite by another. Pan-Asianism (in Ba Maw's words, 'I have heard the voice of Asia calling to her children') has proven to be an empty promise, not only in Burma but elsewhere in Asia, little more than a new twist on colonialism.[66] What sovereignty means is that the different peoples who come together as a nation can develop freely, using their own resources and initiatives as well as those from the outside world, to create a national community that has its own vitality and integrity.[67] As Furnivall suggested, what is needed is a sense of the public interest, of shared citizenship, a 'self to govern itself'.

This requires genuine independence, for if a country becomes the plaything of others in their global strategies, not only do the indigenous people lose control of their politics and economies. They are also deprived of the institutions and practices that have sustained them in the past, without being able to develop viable new ones. Burma's great tragedy is that, because of its geographic location, it was the object of empire-building and top-down social experimentation during both the British colonial and Japanese periods. After the war, it became a lamentable side-show in China's internal political struggles, and arguably today has become, under the auspices of the SPDC junta, a satellite of a Middle Kingdom eager to project its power into the Indian Ocean. The Army-State created by the Burmans was meant to secure the country's sovereignty and independence, but its ethnocentrism has led to protracted civil war and a sell-out to foreign interests. Genuine national unity remains elusive.

Against this background, the question – did the Japanese liberate Burma from colonial rule? – becomes irrelevant, since Burma remains hostage to its own history of ethnic confrontation and the manipulations of its neighbours. True national liberation, *internal* liberation, has not been achieved.

NOTES

[1] *Atarashii Rekishi Kyōkasho* [*New History Textbook*] (2001: 280–281). Both the first and second editions of the middle school textbook, the latter appearing in 2005, have aroused domestic and international criticism for their alleged whitewash of Japan's wartime actions.

[2] Ibid., 282.

[3] Hasegawa (1984: 34, 35).

[4] Hayashi (2001: 9–32).

[5] Hasegawa (1984: 34, 35).

[6] Ibid., 35.

[7] In 1995, when I was living in Malaysia, I noticed that the significance of the 50th anniversary of the war's end was generally felt rather differently by people of Chinese, Indian and Malay descent, due to divergent wartime memories.

[8] McCrae (1990: 76).

[9] The 1935 Government of Burma Act separated Burma administratively from India. It established a bicameral legislature, which like the British parliament chose a prime minister. Most legislators were elected from territorial constituencies, others reserved for minority communities and special interests. The governor, appointed by London, had sole authority over matters relating to defence, finances, foreign relations and the Frontier Areas.

[10] *Thakin* in Burmese means 'master', and Burmese were expected to use it when addressing the British (like *sahib* in India). That young Burmese used the term to refer to themselves had subversive meanings for the colonial regime.

[11] See Guyot (1966: 14, 15) for a list of *Nagani* books by subject matter: eight of a total of 57 dealt with Russia and Marxism, but six each dealt with China and Ireland.

12 Furnivall (1948: 149).

13 Pearn (1939: 287); Saitō and Lee (1999: 15).

14 Furnivall (1948: 111).

15 On 13 April 1919, troops commanded by Brigadier General Reginald Dyer fired at a crowd of peaceful demonstrators in Amritsar, India, killing hundreds; Dyer was never punished, which turned informed Indian public opinion against British rule. See Keay (2000: 475–477).

16 Hall (1960: 172).

17 Ba Maw (1968: 156).

18 One of the engines used on the Thai–Burma Railway is exhibited outside the Yasukuni Shrine in Tokyo, a controversial site strongly associated with pre-1945 Japanese militarism.

19 Seekins (1992: 246–62).

20 'Japanese military totalitarianism could be successfully countered only by our own form of totalitarianism.' Ba Maw (1968: 319).

21 See Guyot (1966: 174–185) and Government of Burma (1943: 1–14).

22 Guyot (1966: 239–245). 'Bureaucrats knew full well they were powerless against the Japanese Army' (245).

23 Ibid., 172, 177, 183.

24 'By not joining in the resistance civil servants lost their last, best chance to prove their nationalist bona fides' (Ibid., 401).

25 Hall (1960: 167).

26 Ba Maw (1968: 62–64, 110–13).

27 Aung San Suu Kyi (1991: 17).

28 Izumiya (1985: 23).

29 Aung San in Silverstein (1993: 83).

30 Ba Maw (1968: 119–125).

31 Aung San in Silverstein (1993: 83).

32 Lintner (1999: 527–529).

33 Yoon (1973: 31).

34 Ibid. (1973: 2).

[35] Yoon (1973: 44–46); Ba Maw (1968: 93, 94, 139). The comrades in arms of Burma's old kings customarily took part in this *pacto de sangre*.

[36] Government of Burma (1943: 59).

[37] Thakin Nu (U Nu) (1954: 24, 25).

[38] Government of Burma (1943: 59, 60); U Maung Maung (1989: 45).

[39] U Maung Maung (1989: 84, 85).

[40] Ibid., 42.

[41] As described by Johnson (1962: 55, 56).

[42] According to informants who spoke to this writer in Rangoon in March 2004, Ne Win changed the name of Resistance Day to Armed Forces Day in order to avoid offending Japan, Burma's largest aid donor.

[43] Ba Maw (1968: 269, 270).

[44] See, for example, Aung San's article, 'Burma's challenge', saying that 'pocket armies will not be permitted,' in Silverstein (1993: 156).

[45] Ba Maw (1968: 130).

[46] Houtman (1999: 153).

[47] See, for example, Chao-Tzang Yawnghwe, 'Burma: the Depoliticization of the Political', in Alagappah (1995: 170–192).

[48] Hla Myint (1997: 141).

[49] Smith (1999: 62, 63).

[50] Ba Maw (1968: 195).

[51] Smith (1999: 63).

[52] Ba Maw (1968: 203–259).

[53] According to Bayly and Harper (2005: 167), 600,000 Indians, Anglo-Indians and Anglo-Burmese fled by land and sea to India, of whom as many as 80,000 died. Ba Maw (1968: 200) mentions that about 500,000 Indians fled Burma in 1942.

[54] Government of Burma (1943: 23, 24).

[55] Smith (1999: 63). The Kachins won the name 'amiable assassins' from their admiring British comrades.

[56] Ibid., 100–101.

[57] Ba Maw (1968: 336, 339).

58 Other participants were Jose Laurel, president of the 'independent' Philippines, Subhas Chandra Bose, leader of the Free India government, Thai prince Waithayakorn, Premier Tōjō Hideki, who served as chairman, and Ba Maw himself. See Ba Maw (1968: 336– 47) for a detailed description of personalities and speeches.

59 Ba Maw (1968: 343).

60 U Maung Maung (1989: 81).

61 Ba Maw (1968: 284).

62 Ibid., 279–281.

63 Ibid., 279, 280.

64 Guyot (1966: 399–417).

65 Ibid., 415, 416.

66 For example, in Aceh in western Sumatra, where the people have fought for their independence against the Indonesian Republic just as they fought against the Dutch a hundred years ago.

67 At the February 1947 Panglong Conference, Aung San seems to have understood this concept of sovereignty through his recognition of minority aspirations. But his military successors have viewed sovereignty and national unity as top-down and homogenizing.

Chapter Two

BURMESE AND JAPANESE WAR NARRATIVES

On 4 January 1981, the thirty-third anniversary of Burma's achieve-ment of independence from British rule, President Ne Win awarded the 'Order of Aung San' (*Aung San Tagun*) to seven veterans of the Minami Kikan. The high-ranking decorations were given at the Presidential mansion in Rangoon, with six of the veterans in attendance ('Bo Mogyo', Colonel Suzuki, had passed away in 1967 and the decoration was accepted posthumously by his wife, Suzuki Setsuko).[1] According to a publication of the Ne Win regime, 'among the recipients of the Aung San Tagun Title are Japanese and Burmese citizens who with sincerity helped Burma attain independence.'[2] Official accounts fail to mention that Ne Win needed Japanese good will. Tokyo was giving him a large amount of official development assistance, a vital life-line for his chronically ailing socialist economy. In many ways, the bilateral 'friendship' born of war has proven useful for both Burmese and Japanese elites, while inconvenient facts or minority views are passed over or suppressed. In both countries, war narratives are also primarily inward-looking.

Burma has been a military dictatorship since 1962, and the print media are tightly censored and controlled.[3] Thus, it is relatively easy to discover an 'official' war narrative, one that reflects the regime's worldview. In post-war Japan, the situation is more fluid: informal constraints on publication exist, but war narratives are more diverse, based on individual experiences, and often hotly contested. But with the encouragement of conservative governments and a mass media directed toward pleasing consumers, a dominant (or at least prevailing) narrative has emerged, focusing on the hellish nature of the Burma War and the heroic sacrifices of Japanese soldiers. This is an epic tragedy, given the numbers of men who died, though not necessarily connected the revisionist idea that Japan 'liberated' Asia from white imperialism.

BURMESE WAR MEMORIES: UNITY

As mentioned in Chapter One, the war provided the post-war leadership with a heroic epic of their own, the story of the Thirty Comrades and the foundation of the *Tatmadaw*. In a history textbook for middle school students published in 1987, the 1940–1945 period is divided into two sub-periods: 'the anti-British struggle' of 1940–1942, when Aung San and other nationalists cooperated with the Japanese and the Burma Independence Army was established; and the 'anti-Japanese, anti-fascist struggle' of 1942–1945, which began with the Japanese occupation and the dissolution of the B.I.A. and closed with the uprising of 27 March 1945 and the Allied victory.[4] This perspective has not changed since the State Law and Order Restoration Council (SLORC) seized power in September 1988, but the post-1988 political crisis has cast the war's greatest hero, Aung San, in a rather different light.

Armed Forces Day (formerly Resistance Day) on 27 March has been one of the country's most important holidays since independence, and probably its most important since the SLORC took over.[5] It is the occasion for a large military parade in Resistance Park, just west of the golden Shwe Dagon Pagoda in Rangoon. The junta's Chairman Senior General Than Shwe gives a speech on the nation's need to preserve unity in the struggle against foreign neo-colonialists and domestic traitors. Weeks beforehand, rehearsals of the parade cause Rangoon traffic jams.[6] The event is subject to the regime's usual thoroughgoing attention to security, which may be warranted, since on 27 March 2003 a bomb was set off near government offices in downtown Rangoon, killing two persons.[7]

In 1998, the State Peace and Development Council published a collection of poems, essays and stories in honour of the fifty-first anniversary of Armed Forces Day in 1996, celebrating the heroic role of the *Tatmadaw* in past wars. One piece of doggerel by Aung Soe Min goes:

> *March twenty seventh, month of Tabaung*
> *Brings forth bitter memories of the past;*
> *It was history, written not with sweat*
> *But with blood. Treachery of the past*
> *Reverberated, episoded [sic] reflecting*
> *From the mirror of yesterdays.*
> *Look yonder, yonder...*
> *'Here comes the Tatmadaw marching*
> *The victorious Tatmadaw marching;*
> *Myanmar heroes, fame perpetuating worldwide.*
> *We will solidify our strength*
> *For the victory is ours.'*
> ...
>
> *Planning ahead for future freedom*
> *With Minami Kigan [sic] Aung San joined hands.*
> *Thirty Comrades in secrecy trained.*
> *A nucleus army the forerunner of Tatmadaw.*
> *BIA was thus born.*
> ...
>
> *Under the fascist heels our nation writhed,*
> *BIA changed to BDA and thence to BNA.*
> *Divisive tactics fail to dim our spirit.*
> *When finally we rose in defiance, routing the enemy.*
> *Imbued with patriotism, marched along in unity.*
> *Our Patriotic Bama [Burma, Myanmar] Army.*[8]

Here, the lesson of the war is simple: before the Japanese occupation, the 'imperialist' British dominated the races of Burma by dividing them against each other, and the 'fascist' Japanese did the same thing in 1941–1945. By uniting in a single force, the *Tatmadaw*, the peoples of Burma could drive out first the 'imperialists', then the 'fascists'. The Japanese invader is only one of several historical enemies who have afflicted Burma over the centuries, along with the Chinese and the British.

The view of World War II as one of many episodes in Burma's struggle for national unity and independence has its patriotic distortions: it was the battle-hardened Japanese Army, not the loosely organized Burma Independence Army, who drove the British out in 1941–1942. According to an official publication of the SPDC, 'it was an undeniable fact that the rapid reconquest of Myanmar by the Allied Forces was due to the gallant fighting of the Burma Army.'[9] But ethnic minority guerrillas, especially the Karens, probably played a greater role in Burma's liberation than the Patriotic Burmese Forces. Indeed, *their* war memories are conspicuously ignored. But even within the dominant Burman narrative, there are troublesome contradictions.

Aung San, the 'father' of the *Tatmadaw* is a pivotal figure, who has been compared in official historiography to the great conqueror-kings of the past such as Anawrahta (r. 1044–1077), Bayinnaung (r. 1551–1581) and Alaungpaya (r. 1752–1760). Before 1988, he was *the* national hero. His portrait hung in government offices and schools, and was engraved on the nation's currency notes, the *kyat* (most often, he was shown wearing a Japanese-style uniform). His exploits were celebrated in textbooks and popular history and his statue placed in a central part of Rangoon and in other cities throughout the nation. His name appears in a number of important places in Rangoon: the Bogyoke Aung San Market (formerly Scott Market) on Bogyoke Aung San Road in the city centre; the Aung San Stadium near the central railway station, and Bogyoke Park on the shores of Kandawgyi Lake. The anniversary of the assassination of Aung San and members of his cabinet by a political rival on 19 July 1947 has been observed as Martyrs' Day, and a ceremony is still held annually at the Martyrs' Mausoleum in Rangoon, not far from where the military holds its Armed Forces Day parade.[10]

During the massive pro-democracy demonstrations of 1988, however, students and townspeople took his portrait from government offices and held it aloft as they marched through the streets of Rangoon.[11] At that instant he became a symbol of opposition, and dangerous to a regime that had, for decades, used him for their own purposes.

After Aung San's daughter, the 43-year-old Aung San Suu Kyi, made a speech on the west slope of the Shwe Dagon Pagoda hill to a huge audience on 26 August, describing the popular demonstrations of 1988 as 'the second struggle for national independence', the official war narrative centred on Aung San began to possess a revolutionary overtone that the *Tatmadaw* establishment found increasingly threatening.[12]

By the early 1990s, it became apparent that Aung San – both on his own terms and through his daughter – had been transformed by oppositionists into a revolutionary and even democratic symbol. The junta has responded with two strategies. One is to 'protect' the wartime leader's reputation by suggesting that, were he still alive, he would be scandalized by his daughter's behaviour: 'If only Aung San were alive,' speculated one regime spokesman, 'I do not know whether he would kill or exile his daughter who married an Englishman.'[13] This apparently has had limited success, since the regime has also undertaken what Gustaaf Houtman calls 'Aung San amnesia'.[14] Martyrs' Day celebrations have been down-sized, prominent SPDC leaders conspicuous in their absence, his portrait removed from post-1988 currency, and his historical role in wartime and post-war Burma not so much erased (as was the case of Trotsky in Stalinist Russia) as marginalized. For example, he is not mentioned at all in Senior General Than Shwe's annual Armed Forces Day speeches.[15] While the junta has built new museums celebrating a 'correct' view of history and the central historical role of the *Tatmadaw*, the Bogyoke Museum, the house where he lived during 1945–1947, is closed down most of the year.[16]

These tactics have left the SLORC/SPDC in a difficult position. Conspicuously lacking heroic qualities and dogged by scandal, Aung San's wartime comrade Ne Win never aspired to his prominence even during the years when he was Burma's dictator.[17] No effort was made after 1988 to promote him as an alternative war hero. The exposure of a so-called 'coup d'état attempt' in early 2002, allegedly plotted by Ne Win's son-in-law and three grandsons, cast a further cloud on his reputation. When the retired dictator died on 5 December 2002, there was no state funeral and his passing was only briefly mentioned in the state-run media.

Thus, the second Army-State has found itself deprived of war heroes, diminishing the 'meaning' of the war in their agenda. Armed Forces Day remains important, but the junta has reached further back in history to harvest militant national heroes. One of their favourites has been Bayinnaung, the ferocious sixteenth century king who devastated the Shan States and brought Siam to its knees, marching back from the pillaged Siamese capital of Ayutthaya loaded with booty, slaves and four sacred white elephants. The junta has reconstructed part of his Kanbawza Thadi Palace at Pegu, northeast of Rangoon, using fanciful design and concrete rather than teak. His statue glowers threateningly on the Burmese side of the Thai-Burma border, a conspicuous warning to the old Siamese foe, and his role as Burma's pre-eminent empire-builder is glorified in the state-run media.

If in official historiography before 1988 Aung San was unique, the father of Burma's independence (as well as the *Tatmadaw*), the evolving view after that year has been that he was only *one* of Burma's many militant heroes. Thus he can be, to an extent, ignored. But it is unclear how the essentially irrelevant Bayinnaung can replace him. It is as if a British government in the name of 'law and order' decided to ignore Gladstone and Churchill, and reach back to Edward I for legitimization.

As mentioned, ethnic minority war memories are ignored by the state. But the massacre of Karens by the B.I.A. and Colonel Suzuki in 1942 is part of the official history of the insurgent Karen National Union; their equivalent to 'Bo Mogyo', is Major

Hugh Seagrim, a British officer who organized Karen guerrillas along the Thai-Burma border and gave his life to spare the Karen people Japanese punishment.[18] When Burma becomes democratic and the aspirations of the minorities are fully recognized, a more inclusive war narrative will doubtlessly include the experiences of those who fought on the British side and suffered Japanese (and Burman) persecution. Burmese war narratives will probably reflect more negatively on the Japanese interlude, like their counterparts in Singapore or the Philippines.

In conclusion, the official war narrative has made the Japanese occupation, like earlier wars and invasions, an object lesson in the need for armed vigilance and the unity of Burma's 'national races'. But because Aung San and his daughter have become symbols of the political opposition, war memories pose paradoxes that the post-1988 junta finds difficult to manage.

JAPANESE WAR MEMORIES: TRAGIC LYRICISM

When a Thai International airbus en route to Rangoon was hijacked on 10 November 1990 by two Burmese students carrying bombs made out of soap and wires, Japanese viewers of the NHK evening news learned that of 221 people on board, 41 were compatriots. All but eight of these people were members of two groups of war veterans (*senyū*, 'comrades-in-arms') going to Burma in order to visit the graves and 'console the spirits' (*irei* in Japanese) of their fallen comrades.[19]

The war in Burma exacted a huge toll on the Japanese Imperial Army. According to statistics presented by Louis Allen, 303,501 soldiers were sent to Burma between 1941 and 1945. But of these, only 118,352 were repatriated to Japan in the years following the war. The remaining 185,149, 61 per cent of the total, probably included a handful of survivors who for some reason did not choose or were unable to return home. But the overwhelming majority were war deaths. They included those who died in the March–June 1944 Imphal Campaign in northeastern India as well as those who fought in the futile defence of Burma against Allied offensives in late 1944–1945. According to Allen's statistics, the Japanese lost only 2,000 men in the 1941–1942 invasion. The great majority of deaths (which were one twelfth of all fatalities suffered by the Japanese in World War II) occurred in the 19-month period between March 1944 (the beginning of the Imphal operation) and September 1945 (the formal Japanese surrender).[20] To put this in perspective, the probable fatality figure of around 185,000 is over three times the number of deaths suffered by the United States in the Indochina War (58,000), which occurred over a period of fifteen years.

The high death figures reflected not only the intensity of the fighting and a harsh physical environment (especially during the monsoon), but the incompetence and lack of planning of the Japanese top command. Inspired by the example of Genghis Khan, General Mutaguchi Renya, commander of the Imphal Campaign, ordered that his troops' main supply of food would be carried on the backs of 20,000 oxen, which, when the rations were exhausted, would then be consumed.[21] But most of the oxen couldn't make it up steep mountain trails, and often got in the way of soldiers on the march. Soldiers lacked food, equipment and even bullets, and were expected to triumph over better-equipped Allied forces on the basis of will power (*Yamato damashii*, 'Japanese spirit') alone.

Like soldiers of other countries and times, care for the remains of fallen comrades was a matter of personal honour. In the midst of battle, men sometimes cut off the finger of a dead soldier so that it could be cremated, and the remains returned to families in Japan.[22] After Burma and Japan established formal diplomatic relations, groups of war veterans visited the country on a regular basis to find the remains of the fallen, offer prayers, and build monuments.

According to one Asian diplomat, among all Japanese veterans of World War II, those who fought in Burma formed the largest and most active groups, visiting the country most frequently in the late 1980s and early 1990s.[23] The search for remains took them to remote parts of the country where major battles were fought, presenting major logistical problems because of the poorly developed infrastructure. During the Ne Win era (1962–1988), Burma was largely isolated from the outside world; tourists were few, and of the Japanese who visited the country, seventy to eighty percent were on 'battlefield tours' (*senseki tsūa*) or 'travel to console the souls of the fallen' (*irei no ryo*). The war monuments were built with Japanese money and design and ceremonies held with high-ranking Japanese officials in attendance. According to one critical Japanese account, the Burmese government was hard pressed to accommodate these visitors and their demands, and local populations witnessing the memorial observances found themselves bystanders in their own land.[24]

But there is another, less inward-looking theme in Japanese war narratives. In the closing days of the war, as soldiers retreated before the Allied onslaught toward the border with Thailand, many were given food and medicine by Burmese villagers. Veterans have returned to the country in the spirit of *ongaeshi* (Japanese, 'gratitude') to assist with grass-roots development projects such as irrigation.[25] It is hard to imagine any other Asian country, with the possible exception of Indonesia, where war memories are tinged with such feelings of good will.

In a 1987 article, Tanabe Hisao writes that he was able to identify 500 books relating to the Burma War by veterans, including both the histories of military units and personal recollections. He attributes the large number of books to the generally friendly relations between Japanese soldiers and the local population during 1942–1945 (the depredations of the *Kempeitai* being an exception); the fact that from late 1942 to mid-1944, conditions were generally peaceful inside Burma, allowing for social interactions; and the vivid memories created by the terrible battles of 1944–1945. The Burma War is often described as *jigoku sen* (hellish war). Among the most influential works were *Ahlone shūyōjo* (translated into English as *Prisoner of the British*), acerbic reflections on the shortcomings of 'western humanism' written by an eminent professor at Kyoto University, Aida Yuji, who after the surrender had been interned by the British at a camp in Rangoon; and *The White Field* by

Furuyama Komao, a fictional work based on his war experiences which won the prestigious Akutagawa Prize in the 1970s.[26]

Some of the memoirs are disarmingly frank, and lend little support to a glorification of the 'Greater East Asia War'. One private, participating in the Imphal Campaign, wrote:

> We complained bitterly to one another of the incompetence of our generals who had sent us into the mountains without any proper climbing equipment or clothing, and hampered by large herds of cattle which could not climb the steep, rocky paths which even we soldiers found hard enough. To make matters worse, medical orderlies had to do their best to walk alongside the sick and wounded, slipping, sliding, falling, time and time again.[27]

Mention Burma to most Japanese, especially the older generation, and they'll think of Takeyama Michio's 1946 novel, *Harp of Burma* [*Biruma no Tategoto*]. One of post-war Japan's great best-sellers, it was made into popular film versions in 1956 and 1985 by the distinguished director Ichikawa Kon. It tells of a company of soldiers who have fought through the Burma campaign and are retreating to the Thai border. Though ill and starving, they are a cheerful group, their morale buoyed by choral singing led by their captain, a music college graduate. The novel's protagonist, Corporal Mizushima, has taught himself the Burmese harp (the country's most representative music instrument), and his favourite tune is *Hanyū no Yado* (the Japanese version of *Home Sweet Home*). In one climactic scene, which according to one's taste will seem either moving or mawkish, the company finds itself surrounded by British troops. As they prepare for battle, Mizushima plays *Hanyū no Yado* on his harp. Before bullets fly, the astonished Japanese soldiers hear the British singing *Home Sweet Home* in English: it turns out the war is over, and the two groups come together in the tropical night and exchange fond memories of home and family.

The soldiers are interned, and Mizushima volunteers to persuade a group of holdouts on a mountainside near the Thai border to surrender. They refuse to give up, calling Mizushima a disgraceful coward, even though the sacrifice of their lives is meaningless now that the war is over. One of the most powerful episodes in the book, the argument between Mizushima and the unit commander shows the absurdity of militarism (Mizushima is also surprised to discover that many of the soldiers holed up on the mountainside are drunk on *sake*). He is wounded in the ensuing battle, is captured by a tribe of 'kachins', and narrowly escapes being cooked and eaten. His harp playing convinces the tribesmen that he has the power to communicate with the *nats* (spirits). They release him and give him the robes of a Buddhist monk.

On the way south to rejoin his fellow soldiers at a camp in Mudon in southern Burma, he discovers the abandoned remains of Japanese soldiers, which he cremates. Encountering another group of rotting corpses by a riverbank, he is revolted, and runs away. But when he sees the British holding a service in Mudon for 'unknown Japanese soldiers', Mizushima realizes what his duty is: not to return home with his comrades and help rebuild his country, but to give the Japanese war dead a proper interment. A 'fierce voice' whispers to him:

> You cannot leave the bones of your comrades to weather by the Sittang River, and in mountains, forests and valleys that you have yet to see! *Hanyū No Yado* is not only a song of yearning for your own home, for your own friends. That harp expresses the longing of every man for the peace of his home. How would they feel to hear it, the dead whose corpses are left exposed in a foreign land? Can you go away from this country without finding some sort of resting place for them? Can you leave Burma? Go back! Retrace your steps! Think over what you have seen on your way here. Or do you just want to leave? Do you lack the courage to go back north?[28]

Mizushima returns to the riverbank and buries the corpses. He decides to live in Burma for the rest of his life as a monk, and doesn't join his fellow soldiers when they are repatriated to Japan.

Written when war memories were fresh, *Harp of Burma* is an anti-war, or at least anti-militarist, book, anticipating the idealistic pacifism of Article 9 of the Japanese Constitution. It is also devoid of a 'dark' perspective, which makes it an uplifting work, but not especially evocative of the realities of war, in the manner, say, of Ōoka Shōhei's *Fires on the Plain* (*Nobi*), with its accounts of cannibalism and despair in the wartime Philippines. The folly and illusion of war are repeatedly stressed, but none of Takeyama's characters raise the issue of who was responsible for starting it. The closest they come is the incident between Mizushima and the holdouts on the mountainside, who seem to be possessed by the drunken madness of war (and *sake*). There is little connection, then, between his work and the great debate over the transformation of 'feudal' values that took place among Japanese just after the war. *Harp of Burma* is not only sentimental, but also resolutely apolitical.

The book is sometimes criticized because Takeyama, unlike George Orwell (whose *Burmese Days* was inspired by his service as a colonial police officer), had never been to Burma. He was a college professor, and apparently gleaned the wartime experiences of some of his students. His book is fuzzy on Burmese geography and customs: for example, there were no cannibals on the Thailand–Burma border, where the episode with the 'kachins' takes place (the Kachins, anyway, live near the China–Burma border), and it is highly unlikely that Burmese villagers would have invited Mizushima, disguised as a high ranking *pongyi* (Buddhist monk), to help gather the bones of the deceased at a cremation ceremony (this custom is Japanese, and carried out by family members).[29]

Takeyama paints an idealized picture of the Burmese as a peaceful, spiritual people, and Mizushima's comrades argue over the relative benefits of the 'civilization' adopted by Japan, with its harsh discipline and modern technology, and the gentle indolence of the Buddhist Burmese: 'The Burmese never seem to have committed our stupid blunder of attacking others.'[30] But no one who is familiar with Burma's history could conclude that they are a peaceful people. Old Burmese kings like Bayinnaung carried out frequent invasions of Siam, Laos and even India, not to mention states like Arakan and Hanthawaddy (Pegu), which were ruled by ethnic minorities now included within the Union of Myanmar.

Colonel Suzuki's great success with the Thirty Comrades was due largely to his understanding of Burmese (or Burman) military traditions, which the British colonialists tried unsuccessfully to stifle.

In fact, *Harp of Burma* has little connection with Burmese people. There is only one Burmese character of even minor importance, an old pedlar woman who speaks Japanese with an Osaka accent and helps Mizushima's comrades locate him. She has a supporting role in a drama whose protagonists are all Japanese. Given its main themes, the longing for peace and comradeship of soldiers that transcends even death, the drama, with minor alterations, could have taken place in any of the battlefields of the Pacific War.

That is, apart from the fact that Burma, like Japan, is a Buddhist country. Takeyama shared with many of his countrymen, including many war veterans, a sense of nostalgic longing about Burmese religion: once, Japan too was suffused with Buddhist values, but lost them in the process of modernization and westernization. By looking at Burma, some Japanese feel they are looking at their own sadly departed past.

The mission that Mizushima's 'fierce voice' charges him with, burying the remains of the war dead, has little connection with Burmese Buddhism. There is a form of Theravada meditation that involves contemplation of corpses, often practised in a cemetery. Its purpose is to achieve spiritual awareness through an appreciation of the repulsiveness of the human body (the 'nine apertures' which exude filthy substances).[31] But however admirable it may be, Mizushima's motive is quite different: he seeks to fulfil the obligation which the living have to the dead, an obligation that transcends the boundaries of the living world, but is still a *social* obligation, much like ancestor worship. Thus Takeyama has taken the outward appearance of Theravada Buddhism, Mizushima's transformation into a *pongyi* and the respectful treatment he receives from Burmese villagers, and turns it into an expression of Japanese (Buddhist) values. This is in itself not necessarily illegitimate, given the terrible sacrifices Japanese soldiers endured during the war, but it shows that it would be a mistake to say that *Harp of Burma* is a book 'about' Burma, in the same way that Orwell's *Burmese Days*, however unflattering, is. There is no equivalent of the shallow and mercenary concubine Ma Hla May, or the malevolent magistrate U Po Kyin, who are unattractive characters, but very convincing.

The men in Mizushima's company enjoy close and harmonious relations, and feel great loss when they learn that he is alive but cannot go back with them to Japan. As mentioned, Takeyama describes the cheerfulness and good morale of the company, due to their practice of singing together. *Harp of Burma* celebrates group life, probably the single most important value in post-war Japanese schools and companies, holding up the relationships of the men as an ideal that other Japanese, in peacetime, can emulate.[32] This is not the brutal uniformity of the army, but an allegedly more benevolent kind of collectivism in which the individuality (*kosei*) of group members is appreciated for promoting group cohesiveness.[33] In the context of his unit, Mizushima is an eccentric character (for example, he often dresses in a *longyi*, a Burmese sarong, and looks Burmese); but everyone likes him for his conscientiousness and his harp playing.

As is often the case, narratives about exotic places and peoples, whether in the form of memoirs or novels, are reflections of the Self rather than the Other. They are inward-looking, leaving the Other without the opportunity to express himself or herself, what Edward Said has called 'Orientalism'. But the positive image generated by Japanese writers about Burma, combined with memories of terrible sacrifice – epitomized by *Harp of Burma* – not only aided the construction of a new, collectively 'peace-loving' Japanese national identity but also laid the foundations for a unique 'friendship' which flourished after diplomatic relations between Japan and the Union of Burma were established in the 1950s.

NOTES

1   An exhibit devoted to this event is kept in the Yūshukan, the museum of the Yasukuni Shrine in Tokyo.

2   *Facts about Burma* (1983: 157).

3   The Press Scrutiny Board was established by the Ne Win regime and still exercises strict censorship of the print media.

4   Koshida (1991: 120–129).

5   In November 1997, the SLORC change its name to the more agreeable sounding State Peace and Development Council (SPDC), with some change in personnel.

6   In 2005, the SPDC relocated Burma's capital from Rangoon to Pyinmana, in the central part of the country. Starting in 2006, the Armed Forces Day celebrations are now held in Pyinmana.

7   *The Irrawaddy* on-line (2003).

8   Aung Soe Min, in *Armed Forces Day* (1998: 45). His poem, titled 'The Trail of the Blazing Stars', won First Prize in a SPDC competition celebrating Armed Forces Day. Tabaung is a month in the Burmese calendar, roughly corresponding to March.

9   *Brief History of the Myanmar Army* (1999: 8).

10 The official depiction of Aung San is of course selective, focusing on his wartime exploits; his earlier career as a student leader is largely passed over.

11 Lintner (1989: 132, 133).

12 Aung San Suu Kyi (1995: 193).

13 Houtman (1999: 31). Daw Suu Kyi's marriage to British academic Michael Aris was used by the regime to claim that she is a race-traitor.

14 Ibid., 26, 27.

15 Ko Jay (2005).

16 According to informants with whom this author talked in Rangoon in March 2004, the Bogyoke Museum is open only for a few days around Martyrs Day in July. During the mid-1990s, the SLORC built a new National Museum and Defence Services Museum. Both devote minimal space to the historical role of Aung San.

17 Indeed, a major reason why the SLORC put Daw Suu Kyi under house arrest in July 1989 seems to have been her promise to reveal

embarrassing details about the less than harmonious relationship between her father and Ne Win, whom he apparently never trusted. In his book *Burma and General Ne Win*, Dr. Maung Maung, his official biographer, described Ne Win as faithfully carrying out Aung San's mandate of preserving national unity.

[18] After Seagrim had established his guerrilla base in the Karen hills, the Japanese caused such a reign of terror among the Karens searching for it that he voluntarily gave himself up, and was executed in September 1944. His story is told by Ian Morrison in *Grandfather Longlegs*.

[19] NHK (Nihon Hōsō Kyōkai) evening news, 10 November 1990. The two groups were the 'Biruma kantetsu doppo tai' [the Walking Company Going Around (Penetrating) Burma] and the 'Biruma–Tai Irei Jumpai no Ryo' [Burma–Thailand Pilgrimage to Console the Spirits of the Dead].

[20] Allen (1984: 637–641). He also gives a lower figure, based on estimated deaths in specific battles and campaigns, of 106,144. But this was still 35 per cent of total Japanese forces in Burma. British and Commonwealth battle and other deaths in Burma were 14,326.

[21] Tamayama and Nunneley (2001: 189). In fact, only 1,000 oxen were obtained.

[22] Ibid., 163.

[23] Comment of Asian diplomat to author, Rangoon, March 1991. Their British counterparts are equally active, through the Burma Star Association.

[24] Tanabe and Utsumi (1990: 189–192). In a similar manner, the American government's determination to find the remains of Indochina War dead has brought forensic teams to remote parts of Vietnam and Laos.

[25] *Asahi Shimbun* (1992).

[26] Tanabe (1987: 308–312). See also Guyot (2001: 87–100) on a comparison of veterans' memoirs from Burma and Indonesia.

[27] Tamayama and Nunneley (2001: 175).

[28] Takeyama (1966: 123).

[29] Ibid., p. 116. For Burmese funeral customs, see Spiro (1982: 248–254).

[30] Takeyama (1966: 48).

31 Spiro (1982: 50). This practice seems to be relatively rare in Burmese Buddhism, but is, or was, widely practiced among Tibetan Buddhists.

32 Whether this was Takeyama's intention is unclear, but after its publication the book became part of the school curriculum.

33 Japanese often say that while *kosei*, 'individuality', is good if it contributes to group goals, *kojinshugi*, 'individualism', is bad because it selfishly undermines the coherence of the group.

Chapter Three

BIRU-KICHI: BURMA–JAPAN RELATIONS AND THE POLITICS OF AID, 1951–1988

Japan was occupied by the Allied powers between 28 August 1945, when the first American troops arrived in the country, and 28 April 1952, when the San Francisco Treaty of 8 September 1951 went into effect and the country recovered its independence. Representatives of Japan and 47 other nations signed the peace treaty. But the Union of Burma, which had achieved independence from British colonial rule on 4 January 1948, did not send a representative.[1] Like his neighbour and close friend Jawaharlal Nehru of India, who also boycotted the conference, Burma's Prime Minister U Nu thought that the United States, which as Japan's major occupier controlled the treaty proceedings, planned to use Japan as a base against the Soviet Union and its socialist allies. Signing the treaty would have violated his commitment to non-aligned neutrality. Moreover, Burma and other Asian nations that had suffered from wartime devastation wanted adequate reparations from Tokyo, while Washington used the treaty to shield its new Cold War protégé from crippling indemnities.[2] By working from outside the San Francisco treaty framework, U Nu had a freer hand in negotiating a separate peace with Japan's Prime Minister, Yoshida Shigeru.

Even before formal diplomatic ties were established, the Japanese government opened an overseas office (Japanese, *zai gai jimusho*) in the Burmese capital in November 1951, which was upgraded to a consulate-general (*sōryōjikan*) in April of the following year. In May 1953, the government of Burma opened a consulate-general in Tokyo. On 4 November 1954, the two countries signed a peace treaty and an agreement on war reparations, which went into effect in April of 1955. By this time, both countries had full-fledged embassies in their respective capitals, and relations were fully normalized.[3]

After the war, Japan's agricultural sector was in disarray, and Burma provided the country with rice: over 300,000 tons in 1954 alone.[4] It is a little known fact that for a time in the 1950s, Japan was the world's largest importer of rice. This was before Tokyo's policy of rice self-sufficiency was put in place under Liberal Democratic Party rule, to achieve food security and win the farm vote. By 1960, rice had become a bilateral trade issue, not only due to declining imports overall but also because the Burmese believed that Japan was discriminating against Burmese rice, in favour of other importers.[5]

Although wartime friendships continued after 1945, the post-war relationship reflected economic rather than military or political priorities. Japan was no longer a military power, but following the boom created by the outbreak of the Korean War in 1950, it rapidly transformed itself into a dynamic engine of economic growth. After war reparations payments were begun in 1955, Japan became Burma's largest donor of development assistance. By the 1970s, a substantial community of interests had emerged between policymakers in Tokyo, concerned with short-term satisfaction of politically powerful business constituencies and long-term economic strategies in Southeast Asia, and President Ne Win and his subordinates in Rangoon, who needed inflows of foreign capital, but not at the price of effectively opening up Burma's socialist and military-controlled economy. The relationship encountered difficulties before 1988, but that year marked a turning point as Tokyo temporarily halted aid flows for political reasons.

WAR REPARATIONS

The agreement for war reparations (Japanese, *baishō*), the first made by Japan with any Asian country, committed Tokyo to providing Rangoon with US$250 million over the 1955–1965 period: US$200 million, to be paid out in annual instalments of US$20 million, for goods and services provided by the Japanese government; and an additional US$50 million, in annual instalments of US$5 million, for technical assistance and investment in joint ventures between Japanese private firms and the Burmese public and private sector.[6] Although their purpose was to compensate Burma for damage and suffering caused by the 1941–1945 occupation, reparations created markets for Japanese goods and services in Burma and other Southeast Asian countries during the 1950s and 1960s at a time when Japan was rebuilding its own economy. According to Marie Söderberg, 'Money was "tied" and rather than aid, it can be regarded as the promotion of exports from Japanese industry.'[7]

Included in the original agreement was an 'equality clause' stating that additional funds would be provided by Japan if the amount of reparations given to other countries was larger than that given to Burma. Since this was the case (a 1956 agreement with the Philippines gave it a total of US$770 million, and one with Indonesia US$220.0 million plus the cancellation of an almost equally large amount of debt), a new Rangoon–Tokyo agreement in 1963 provided for an additional US$140 million in so-called 'quasi-reparations' (*jun-baishō*), grant aid to be paid out during the 1965–1977 period.

The question of additional reparation funds strained relations between the two countries. In 1959, Tokyo, which had just concluded a reparations agreement with South Vietnam, said that it could grant no more than US$50 million in additional funds to Burma. The Caretaker Government of General Ne Win reacted by imposing an embargo on Japanese goods and threatening to cancel the visas of Japanese businessmen resident in the country. According to a correspondent for the *Far Eastern Economic Review*, the Japanese Ministry of Finance feared a flood of new indemnity claims from Asian countries, while the Foreign Ministry and Ministry of International Trade and Industry were more receptive to Burma's requests. He writes that 'some civilians close to the Government believe that the military [the Caretaker Government] has been too abrupt and crude in its boycott, and that negotiations should be commenced to reach compromise on both trade [Burmese rice imports] and reparations. But the belief that Burma is being hard done by is shared by all.'[8]

The matter was not completely settled until January 1963 when Brigadier Aung Gyi, a member of General Ne Win's Revolutionary Council (the formal name of Burma's first military junta), led a team of negotiators to Tokyo. In his words: 'We [the Burmese] have come here as a younger brother would to an older brother to consult [on] a certain family problem.' According to David Steinberg, his subservience may have angered Ne Win, and contributed, along with differences concerning economic policy, to his resignation from the Revolutionary Council on 7 February 1963.[9] Tokyo allocated the first official development assistance (ODA) funds not associated with reparations or quasi-reparations in 1968, while quasi-reparations were still being paid out.[10]

Retired Japanese officials who had been active in aid relations, interviewed by this writer, claim that compared with Indonesia and the Philippines, the Burmese government used the reparation funds with a minimum of corruption. The modesty of the initial Burmese demand for reparations also impressed them.[11] In *Economic Development in Burma: 1951–1960*, Louis Walinsky, an American economic consultant who worked in Burma, wrote that the government of Prime Minister U Nu chafed at the Japanese government's requirement that all aid contracts with Japanese firms be submitted to it for approval. The Burmese successfully obtained a more flexible arrangement that prevented Tokyo from assuming a 'Big Brother' role by, among other things, arguing from the precedent of the West German–Israeli reparations agreement.[12] Walinsky credits an official of Burma's foreign ministry for negotiating better terms. Along with Burma's reputation for honesty, the incident is worthy of mention because it shows that the newly independent country had competent officials – the inheritors of British civil service professionalism – to advance its interests. Following the overthrow of parliamentary government by Ne Win in March 1962, these professionals were largely purged from the civil service and replaced by military men whose primary qualification was loyalty to Ne Win.[13]

Some observers had rather different opinions about the quality of government under U Nu. One writes: 'A ramified bureaucracy suffocates nearly all economic activity with controls and delays. One small example: the Japanese embassy in Rangoon estimates that it takes six months for a notice of Colombo Plan scholarships to circulate around the various States.'[14] However, many Japanese specialists and officials got the label *Biru-kichi* (from the Japanese words *Biruma* [Burma] and *kichigai* [crazy], i.e., 'Burma crazy') during the reparations period because of their vocal enthusiasm for the country and its people. *Biru-kichi* and the sentiment that the country was the 'friendliest toward Japan in Asia' because of shared wartime history meshed nicely, creating a subjective climate in which the allocation of post-reparations loans and grants on Tokyo's part was strongly encouraged.

The largest reparations-era project, and one that continues to be important at the beginning of the twenty-first century, was the Baluchaung hydroelectric power plant, which was built along the river of the same name, a tributary of the Salween River, in remote Karenni (Kayah) State. The project grew out of a visit to Burma in 1953 by the president of Nippon Kōei, an engineering consulting company that was to play a major role in Japanese ODA in Burma right up to 1988. Reconstituted after the war from the old Yalu River Hydroelectric Company, Nippon Kōei had experience constructing power plants in northern Korea and Manchuria during the Japanese colonial era. The Burmese government was looking for a place to build a hydroelectric plant, to supply Rangoon and cities in central Burma with reliable power, and Japanese experts suggested the Baluchaung site.[15]

It was a formidable undertaking. The countryside is rugged and remote, the river dropped over 2,000 feet (670 metres) through a series of steep waterfalls in the area where construction was planned, and the region was home to groups of Karenni ethnic minority insurgents. Construction began in 1956, the principal Japanese participants being Nippon Kōei and Kajima, a major construction company. During the most active construction phase in the late 1950s, 250 Japanese experts were on the site. The first stage was completed by March 1960 at a cost of US$25 million.[16] Altogether, about 17 per cent of total reparation funds during 1955–1963 were used on the project.[17]

Japanese observers see Baluchaung as one of the great success stories in the five-decade history of Japanese reparations and aid between 1955 and 2005. Through the Ne Win (1962–1988) and State Law and Order Restoration Council/State Peace and Development Council (1988–) eras, the plant, kept under a minimum of repair, has provided Burma's capital with a steady if sometimes low supply of electric power. The aging power plant's renovation was one of the first 'new' aid projects undertaken by Tokyo in a hopeful climate of dialogue between the military junta and Daw Aung San Suu Kyi in 2001–2002.

Less successful were the 'four industrial projects' financed with reparations funds beginning in 1962. Their purpose was to promote Burma's industrialization through the support of assembly plants for the manufacture of light and heavy vehicles, agricultural machinery, and electrical items. Over time, the factories were supposed to become self-sufficient through the increasing use of made-in-Burma components. Four Japanese companies – Hino (truck assembly), Mazda (automobiles, jeeps and vans), Kubota (farm machinery) and Matsushita (electrical appliances) – were given contracts by the Japanese government for the initial supply of components. Though the contracts were profitable for the suppliers, self-sufficiency in parts was never achieved. According to a Japanese embassy report in the 1980s, only 35 per cent of components by value were local. The factories suffered from low productivity and quality, but after 'quasi-reparation' funds for the projects ran out in 1972, ODA in the form of commodity loans continued to support the projects: between 1972 and 1987, these loans were renewed 13 times, a total of ¥140 billion.[18] Procurement contracts for the projects were never opened to competitive bidding, and the four original companies continued to supply the factories with parts. In terms of their expense (they comprised about 35 per cent of total yen loans during 1972–1987) and lack of success in promoting the growth of local manufacturing, the four industrialization projects, closed down amidst much criticism in the late 1980s, seemed a symbol of all that was wrong with Japanese aid policies. [19]

QUANTITY AND QUALITY OF POST-REPARATIONS AID

Under the civilian governments that ruled Burma from 1948 to 1958 and again from 1960 to 1962, and the military 'caretaker' government in power during 1958–1960, Burma was committed to building a socialist economic system. But it had a mixed public-private economy in which there was a large foreign presence: not only foreign aid donors, principally Japan, but also foreign private enterprise and a domestic business class composed chiefly of the descendants of South Asian and Chinese immigrants who had arrived in the country during the British colonial period. The payment of Japanese reparations, however, extended well into the period of rigid, Eastern European-style socialist economic policies under General Ne Win's Revolutionary Council. Between 1962 and 1988, Burma's aid relationship with Japan was unusual for three reasons:

(1)   Although Ne Win-era Burma was a one-party state with a centrally planned economy, capitalist Japan was allowed to play an important economic role through its reparations and ODA.

(2)   In the Burmese case, the aid presence was not supplemented by significant bilateral trade (outside of ODA-driven trade) or Japanese private investment.

(3)   Given the relatively small size and undeveloped nature of the Burmese economy, the amount of Japanese aid was huge, particularly in the ten years preceding the 1988 political crisis. Aid continued to flow on a large scale even when it became evident that the socialist economy had little or no short-term or medium-term promise of development. [20]

Japan provided two thirds of all bilateral (nation-to-nation) ODA disbursements to Burma, amounting to US$1.94 billion in grants and loans between 1970 and 1988 (see Table 3.1 below). Japanese funding was also provided indirectly through multilateral institutions such as the Asian Development Bank, which Burma joined in the 1970s. During the 1970s and 1980s, Burma's second largest donor was the Federal Republic of Germany (West Germany), while third place was occupied by the United States, Canada, Australia and several European countries in different years.[21]

Table 3.1: Japan's official development assistance to Burma (bilateral disbursements), percentage share of Development Assistance Committee (DAC) total, and other major donors, 1970–2001 (millions of U.S. dollars; percentage shares in parentheses)

	1970	1971	1972	1973	1974	1975	1976	1977
Total ODA[1]	20.4	38.2	40.2	66.9	59.9	29.0	39.3	54.7
Japan ODA	11.9	26.7	29.6	56.3	46.4	21.6	27.3	20.6
%-age of total ODA	(58.3)	(69.9)	(73.6)	(84.2)	(77.5)	(74.5)	(69.5)	(37.7)
Japan's rank	1	1	1	1	1	1	1	1
2nd ranking country[2]	FRG	FRG	FRG	FRG	FRG	AUS	FRG	FRG
amount	3.4	6.5	4.5	5.0	6.8	3.0	5.2	9.6
3rd ranking country[2]	USA	CAN	USA	CAN	AUS	FRG	AUS	USA
amount	2.0	2.2	2.0	1.9	4.0	3.0	2.8	9.0

	1978	1979	1980	1981	1982	1983	1984	1985
Total ODA[1]	156.8	259.1	231.3	203.4	208.0	215.7	148.7	253.2
Japan ODA	104.0	178.0	152.5	125.4	103.9	113.4	95.4	154.0
%-age of total ODA	(66.3)	(68.7)	(65.9)	(61.7)	(50.0)	(52.6)	(64.2)	(60.8)
Japan's rank	1	1	1	1	1	1	1	1
2nd ranking country[2]	FRG	FRG	FRG	FRG	FRG	FRG	FRG	FRG
amount	15.8	51.8	26.3	30.5	59.7	75.3	25.1	65.0
3rd ranking country[2]	NET	DMK	UK	FRA	AUS	AUS	AUS	USA
amount	13.3	9.9	15.1	12.8	17.2	6.7	8.2	8.0

	1986	1987	1988	1989	1990	1991	1992	1993
Total ODA[1]	307.7	240.7	332.7	89.9	83.1	105.9	82.7	77.3
Japan ODA	244.1	172.0	259.6	71.4	61.3	84.5	72.1	68.6
%-age of total ODA	(79.3)	(71.5)	(78.0)	(79.4)	(73.8)	(79.8)	(87.2)	(88.7)
Japan's rank	1	1	1	1	1	1	1	1
2nd ranking country[2]	FRG	FRG	FRG	FIN	FRA	FRA	FRA	FRA
amount	22.4	25.7	37.1	4.7	9.7	8.0	3.3	3.4
3rd ranking country[2]	USA	USA	USA	FRG	SWI	SWI	FRG	FRG
amount	9.0	11.0	10.0	4.6	2.5	5.1	3.2	1.6

	1994	1995	1996	1997	1998	1999	2000	2001
Total ODA[1]	142.8	126.2	45.3	23.6	27.4	44.7	68.1	89.2
Japan ODA	133.8	114.2	35.2	14.8	16.1	34.2	51.8	69.9
%-age of total ODA	(93.7)	(90.5)	(77.7)	(62.7)	(58.8)	(76.5)	(76.1)	(78.4)
Japan's rank	1	1	1	1	1	1	1	1
2nd ranking country[2]	CAN	FRA	FRA	FRA	NOR	NOR	USA	USA
amount	2.6	4.3	2.1	1.9	2.4	1.9	3.4	2.9
3rd ranking country[2]	FRA	NET	NET	AUS	NET	AUS	NOR	NOR
amount	2.0	2.0	1.8	1.7	1.9	1.9	2.9	2.8

Source: Organization for Economic Cooperation and Development. *Geographical Distribution of Financial Flows to Developing Countries*. Paris: Organization for Economic Cooperation and Development (OECD), volumes covering the years 1969–1975, 1971–1977, 1976–1979, 1978–1981, 1979–1982, 1980–1983, 1981–1984, 1985–1988, 1986–1989, 1987–1990, 1988–1991, 1989–1992, 1990–1993, 1990–1994, 1991–1995, 1992–1996, 1993–1997, 1994–1998, 1995–1999, 1996–2000, 1998–2002, 1999–2003, s.v. Burma/Myanmar.

[1]   Total net bilateral official development assistance (ODA) disbursements from Development Assistance Committee (DAC) countries including grants, technical cooperation and loans. Does not include funds under the 'other official flows' category or from multilateral lenders such as the Asian Development Bank.

[2]   AUS: Australia; CAN: Canada; DMK: Denmark; FIN: Finland; FRG: Federal Republic of Germany (before 1990, West Germany); FRA: France; NET: Netherlands; NOR: Norway; SWI: Switzerland; UK: United Kingdom; USA: United States of America.

During the nine-year 1980–1988 period, Burma consistently ranked among the top ten recipients of Japanese ODA disbursements (see Table 3.1 above and and Table 3.2 on p. 67).[22] In terms of percentages of total bilateral aid given by Japan, Burma's share ranged in the 1978–1988 period from a high of nine per cent in 1979 to a low of 3.3 per cent in 1987. Smaller shares in later years, however, are slices of a bilateral ODA 'pie' which grew from US$1.97 billion in 1979 to US$5.25 billion in 1987 and US$6.42 billion in 1988.[23]

By the early 1980s, the Japanese aid presence included project loans, commodity loans, grant aid, technical assistance, and food aid.[24] Between 1978 and 1988, the loan component of Japanese aid ranged annually from 49 to 90 per cent of the total disbursed. Although the quality of Japanese aid (among other things, the high percentage of loans compared to grants) was frequently criticized at the time, West German aid to Burma also contained a high loan component, between 63 and 93 per cent, during the same period.[25]

The large scale of Japanese aid can perhaps be best appreciated by comparing it to amounts given by Tokyo to other Southeast Asian countries where the local economy was more dynamic and the Japanese private sector more active than in Burma. The US$1.42 billion which was disbursed to Burma in 1980–1988 was 63 per cent of the amount given to Thailand (US$2.42 billion) during the same period, at the time the newest of Asia's 'Newly Industrializing Economies'. The figure is 42 per cent of the amount disbursed to Indonesia (US$3.36 billion), a country of primary importance in Japan's natural resource security strategy, which alternated with the People's Republic of China as the largest recipient of Japanese aid during the 1980s.[26]

Figures on the volume of Japanese aid, however, tell only part of the story. Both sympathetic and critical observers described Japanese ODA in the 1980s as closely linked to the country's trade and private investment in recipient countries. Thailand provides a good example. Levels of Japanese aid, private investment, and bilateral trade were high.[27] The complementary roles played by the Japanese public and private sectors in establishing a new industrial economy were an important factor in the country's growth before the 1997 financial crisis. This would not have occurred, however, if Thai policymakers had not nurtured an environment that was conducive to foreign investment, especially during the 1980s. Another important factor has been the close collaboration of Thai and Thai-Chinese business people with Japanese trading and manufacturing firms. Profitable joint ventures were established which first produced goods for the domestic market, but later exported to other Asian countries and even Japan itself.[28]

There is no Burmese version of this success story. Ne Win's socialist regime not only nationalized foreign firms but closed down domestic private enterprises as well. State corporations were established that controlled practically every aspect of economic life outside the flourishing black market. In all cases, they were wasteful and poorly managed. Opportunities for foreign private investment were almost non-existent. Among the few exceptions were a joint venture established in 1955 with a West German state-owned firm, Fritz Werner, to manufacture small arms and an offshore natural gas exploration project in the Andaman Sea with a Japanese consortium in the early 1980s.[29] Fritz Werner's joint venture continued to operate through the Ne Win era (1962–1988).[30] Overseas Chinese and Indian communities, who have played a central role in development elsewhere in Southeast Asia, were systematically deprived of their role in the economy in the 1960s through nationalization of their enterprises, and even forced to leave the country. Outside of ODA requirements, the languishing Burmese economy provided a miniscule market for Japanese products.

A 'BOOMERANG ECONOMY'?

Why Burma? For the reasons outlined above, the large scale of aid given to Rangoon up to 1988 seems paradoxical, especially after quasi-reparations ran out in the late 1970s. With a stagnating economy, the country did not seem to fit into the familiar pattern of Tokyo's ODA serving as 'seed money' for Japanese private investment in Third World countries.[31] Could it be that personal networks linking war veterans, Japanese politicians, and Ne Win were so influential that Burma received special treatment? This is a difficult question to answer, since while personal connections certainly did exist, they were largely hidden from public view, making their impact unclear.

Table 3.2: Burma's ranking among recipients of Japanese bilateral official development assistance, 1980–88 (millions of US dollars in parentheses show total ODA amount for each country from Japan)

1980	1981	1982
Indonesia (350.0)	Indonesia (299.8)	P. R. China (368.9)
Bangladesh (215.1)	South Korea (295.5)	Indonesia (294.5)
Thailand (189.6)	Thailand (214.5)	Bangladesh (215.8)
BURMA (152.5)	Philippines (210.0)	Thailand (170.3)
Pakistan (112.4)	Bangladesh (144.9)	Philippines (136.4)
Philippines (94.4)	*BURMA* (125.4)	*BURMA* (103.9)
South Korea (76.3)	Pakistan (117.7)	Pakistan (95.3)
Malaysia (65.6)	Egypt (70.7)	Malaysia (75.3)
Nepal (24.3)	Malaysia (64.7)	Egypt (61.6)
Iran (23.1)	Turkey (51.4)	Sri Lanka (61.6)

1983	1984	1985
P. R. China (350.1)	P. R. China (389.4)	P. R. China (387.9)
Thailand (248.1)	Malaysia (245.1)	Thailand (264.1)
Indonesia (235.5)	Thailand (232.0)	Philippines (240.0)
Philippines (147.0)	Indonesia (167.7)	Indonesia (161.3)
India (129.5)	Philippines (160.1)	*BURMA* (154.0)
BURMA (113.4)	Bangladesh (123.3)	Malaysia (125.6)
Bangladesh (104.2)	*BURMA* (95.4)	Bangladesh (121.5)
Malaysia (92.3)	Egypt (81.5)	Pakistan (93.3)
Sri Lanka (73.1)	Pakistan (67.0)	Sri Lanka (83.7)
Pakistan (72.8)	Sri Lanka (63.8)	Egypt (73.0)

1986	1987	1988
P. R. China (497.0)	Indonesia (707.3)	Indonesia (984.9)
Philippines (438.0)	P. R. China (553.1)	P. R. China (673.7)
Thailand (260.4)	Philippines (379.4)	Philippines (534.7)
Bangladesh (248.5)	Bangladesh (334.2)	Thailand (360.6)
BURMA (244.1)	India (303.9)	Bangladesh (342.0)
India (226.7)	Thailand (302.5)	Pakistan (302.2)
Indonesia (160.8)	Malaysia (276.4)	*BURMA* (259.6)
Pakistan (151.6)	*BURMA* (172.0)	Sri Lanka (199.8)
Sri Lanka (126.9)	Pakistan (126.7)	India (179.5)
Egypt (125.7)	Sri Lanka (118.2)	Egypt (172.9)

Source: Japan. Ministry of Foreign Affairs. *Waga Kuni no Seifu Kaihatsu Enjo*, vol. 1. Tokyo: Association for Promotion of International Cooperation, editions of 1987, 1988, 1989, 1990, 1991: graph – 'Waga kuni nikokukan ODA no jutai kyōyo koku, kyōyo kaku [The ten largest recipients of Japanese ODA and the amounts disbursed]'.

We know that influential Japanese politicians, such as Prime Minister Kishi Nobusuke, his adopted son Abe Shintarō, and Watanabe Michio, both powerful L.D.P. faction leaders, took a personal interest in the country.[32] Japanese ambassadors to Rangoon had greater access to Ne Win during his years in power than the representatives of other countries. Also, he continued to meet with members of the old Minami Kikan on a social basis through the 1980s.[33] But Ne Win, though of mixed Chinese-Burmese descent, was intensely xenophobic, distrustful of any kind of foreign presence inside his country. For their part, the Japanese war veterans had limited political influence inside Japan. Along with *biru-kichi* sentimentality, the personal dimension was at best a contributing factor, important only insofar as it operated in tandem with other factors inherent to both the Japanese and Burmese political systems. While long-standing personal ties have played an important role in the bilateral relationship, large aid disbursements are best understood as reflecting the mutually beneficial *symbiosis* of two rather different polities.

In the wake of the 1988 political crisis, Japanese journalists and academics held up Burma as a worst case of aid mismanagement. In the words of a June 1989 *Mainichi Shimbun* editorial, Burmese ODA was *tarenagashi*, a term implying an unregulated flow (of funds) without concern for the consequences.[34] The commodity loans for the four industrial projects, as mentioned above, were the most striking example. Though they failed to achieve their purpose, promotion of Burma's industrial self-sufficiency, they were renewed 13 times for a total of ¥140.0 billion, and the same four companies continued to receive lucrative procurement contracts until the loans were finally discontinued in 1987.

According to economist Saitō Teruko, Japanese aid to the Ne Win regime was minimally effective in raising the living standards of the Burmese people, designed to create markets for Japanese companies through procurement contracts, concerned with building huge, costly projects which were often inappropriate in terms of Burma's low level of technology, and regionally biased.[35] She criticized policymakers for not allowing full public access to information on how ODA funds were used, and also commented that project evaluation, carried out by the Japanese Ministry of Foreign Affairs, the embassy staff, and the Japan International Cooperation Agency (JICA), did not include impartial third parties. Indeed, the Ne Win regime disliked any attempt at project evaluation.[36]

The criticism that Japanese aid favours large projects is borne out by statistics published by JICA (see Table 3.3, next page). The biggest percentages of grants and loans disbursed between 1978 and 1987 were in the mining, manufacturing and energy sectors, public works, and commodity loans. The statistics show that small percentages of ODA were spent on human resources and health. Nothing falls under the category of social welfare. The average cost of 69 projects was ¥4.5 billion (at the 1987 exchange rate of US$1.00=¥144.64, this was equivalent to US$31.2 million).[37]

The JICA sources also substantiate the charge that aid projects tended to be regionally biased. Most were concentrated in the central part of the country where the majority Burman ethnic group lives (an important exception, for technical reasons, is the Baluchaung hydroelectric power plant, located in an area where Karenni guerrillas operate). [38] This should not be surprising, however, given the fact that Burmans have monopolized political power since independence in 1948 and many of the ethnic minorities have carried out long-running insurgencies against the central government.[39]

The Nihon–Biruma Kyōkai (Japan–Burma Association) provided aid critics with a smoking gun on 25 January 1989 when this long-established business group presented a petition to the Japanese government requesting the restoration of formal diplomatic relations and the resumption of aid flows, which had been frozen in the wake of the instability and the violent suppression of the pro-democracy movement in 1988. Two of the reasons cited in the petition were the large financial losses which would be suffered by Japanese companies working on ODA projects if aid were indefinitely suspended, and the possibility that Japan's economic withdrawal from Burma would make it possible for other Asian nations such as Singapore and South Korea to gain a dominant position in the country's post-socialist economy.[40]

Table 3.3: Japanese Aid to Burma by Sector, 1978–1987 (unit: yen one billion)

Sector	Amount	% of total	Average cost of projects (number)[1]
Planning, administration	0.9 bn	0.3%	0.9 bn (1)
Public utilities, public works	65.7 bn	21.2%	4.4 bn (15)
Agriculture, fishing	58.4 bn	18.9%	3.4 bn (17)
Mining, manufacturing, energy	87.2 bn	28.2%	5.4 bn (16)
Commerce, travel, industry	0	0%	0
Human resources	6.9 bn	2.2%	0.9 bn (8)
Health, medicine	8.3 bn	2.7%	1.0 bn (8)
Social welfare	0	0%	0
Commodity loans	79.0 bn	25.5%	7.2 bn (11)
Other	82.0 bn	26.5%	20.5 bn (4)
TOTAL	309.4 bn	100.0%	4.5 bn (69)

Source: Japan International Cooperation Agency (JICA). *Keizai Gijutsu kyōryoku kokubetsu shiryō: Biruma*. Series no. 79. Tokyo: JICA, September 1989, pp. 19–38.

[1]   Number of projects per sector in parentheses

Included in the petition was a list of loan and grant aid projects affected by the freeze. Funding for these projects totalled ¥65.9 billion, of which ¥36.9 billion had not been released to the contractors by the Japanese government because of the ODA freeze (using the 1988 average exchange rate of US$1.00=¥128.15, these sums were US$514 million and US$288 million, respectively).[41] The Association's membership in the late 1980s was a Who's Who of the Japanese business world. It included chairmen of the board of 14 of Japan's largest companies such as Mitsubishi Shōji, Mitsui Bussan, Sumitomo Shōji, Nishō Iwai, Mitsubishi Petroleum, Mitsubishi Heavy Industries, Kashima Construction Company, Tōmen, and Kanematsu Gōshō, as well as 36 other corporate members.[42]

The central importance given in Japanese ODA to large-scale and infrastructure projects is reflected in the Nihon–Biruma

Kyōkai's list of projects for which funds had been frozen in 1988. The largest amount was modernization of Rangoon's international airport at Mingaladon (¥12.2 billion out of a total of ¥14.2 billion frozen, or US$95.2 million out of US$110.8 million), followed by consultant contracts and maintenance of the Baluchaung power plant (¥5.7 billion, out of ¥12.7 billion, or US$44.5 million out of US$99.1 million), a caustic soda plant at Kyaiklat, near Rangoon (¥5.2 billion, or US$40.6 million, all of which had been frozen), and a gas turbine generator at Rangoon (¥4.07 billion, out of ¥4.5 billion, or US$31.8 million out of US$35.1 million).[43]

Given the Japanese business world's interest in Burma, it may not be unfair to consider Tokyo's aid presence there in the 1970s and 1980s as an example of what economist Kakazu Hiroshi, in another context, has called a 'boomerang economy'. In his words, 'The term implies that since most financial assistance is tied to the country which provides the assistance, benefits of the assistance are returned to the donor country through imports from the donor.'[44] Because the parties involved in aid projects wished to maximize their own benefit by generating larger and more ambitious projects, there were strong pressures to relegate local needs to a secondary status in decision-making. The result was, as Professor Saitō and other critics write, large projects that were less than fully appropriate to the Burmese context and which were also likely to be overpriced.

During the period in question, the boomerang effect was exacerbated by institutional factors in aid policy formation. First, there was the decentralized and consensus-oriented nature of Japanese ODA decision-making. Not one but three major and one minor government agencies were involved in aid policy: the Ministry of Finance, the Ministry of Foreign Affairs, the Ministry of International Trade and Industry, and the Economic Planning Agency.[45] In addition, as many as sixteen other Japanese government agencies had some input into the ODA decision-making process.[46] Secondly, staff shortages, both in Tokyo and in the field, limited the ability of aid officials to act decisively even as the amount of money allocated to ODA grew rapidly during the late 1970s and

1980s. Overburdened aid officials found themselves having to rely on information provided by Japanese corporations working in recipient countries, or even by foreign government agencies such as the United States Agency for International Development.[47]

Moreover, the Diet's minimal role in deciding the quantity and quality of aid allocations to recipient countries tended to insulate bureaucrats, engineering consultants and business people from public scrutiny.[48] Japan's parliament has held only brief and intermittent debates on Burma ODA. In 1989, foreign ministry officials were questioned concerning newspaper reports that components supplied for the four industrialization projects were used to build trucks for use by the military, a violation of the government's principle that Japanese aid should never be diverted to military purposes. According to the *Mainichi Shimbun*, the Hino assembly plant produced 25,000 units during the time the project was funded, 6.5-ton models, the exact same truck used by the military.[49] Despite regime assertions to the contrary, there was considerable evidence that the allegations were true. Yet there was no follow up by the Diet.[50]

Another important factor in the large volume of aid was the approval of ODA projects on the basis of 'requests' from recipient countries (called *yōsei shugi*, literally 'request-ism', in Japanese) rather than the donor country's strategic or comprehensive development plans. The system seems to have emerged in response to Asian fears that Japan might use aid money to interfere in their internal affairs (war memories were still fresh); but in practice, governments making the requests were often dependent on Japanese consultants to draw up project specifications, providing the major engineering consultant firms with much if not most of their business.[51] Although in the 1980s Japan had a lower percentage of formally tied aid than other donors (most grant contracts had to be awarded to Japanese firms, but non-Japanese firms could compete for loan project contracts), the 'request based' system gave Japanese engineering consultant firms such as Nippon Kōei a major if not principal role in designing project proposals.[52] Thus, they could informally tie projects to certain Japanese suppliers even when bidding was open to non-Japanese firms as well. Competing Japanese suppliers, hungry for procurement contracts, lobbied the consultant firms intensely in order to secure a favoured position before the bidding process began (one writer described them as resembling 'emperors', *tennō*, of the contract bidding process).[53]

Finally, the distinct characteristics of the Burmese political and administrative environment should be taken into consideration. As mentioned above, Ne Win purged competent, professional civil servants. Thus, the formulation of aid requests in tandem with Japanese consultants was likely to have had minimum constructive input from the Burmese side. Also, the autocratic nature of Ne Win's state, his personalistic style of rule, and deteriorating levels of public education and political consciousness (the emasculation of Burma's once excellent universities, the closing down of high quality vernacular and English language newspapers such as *The Nation* in favour of simplistic propaganda sheets such as the government-controlled *Working People's Daily*) – not to mention the high personal costs of criticizing the regime, given the pervasive presence of the much-feared Military Intelligence Service – meant that there was no monitoring of Japanese aid by officials, journalists, intellectuals, or members of the public in the recipient country. The situation contrasted sharply with the Philippines, Thailand and even Indonesia where Japanese aid has been a focus of controversy since the 1970s.

In the case of Burma, the environment in which decisions about ODA commitments were made was characterized by substantial economic interests, a mostly closed circle of planners and bidders who remained largely the same over a long period of time, intense competition among these parties for contracts, lack of legislative (Diet) oversight, lack of effective monitoring by other parties, and the recipient country's lack of initiative in determining the best use of ODA funds to achieve economic development (despite the formal emphasis on *yōsei shugi*). It also illustrated the problem of keeping aid programs – in principle designed to raise the living standards and productivity of people in recipient countries – uncontaminated by commercial interests. And most basically, it showed that governments with money to spend (or money to borrow) often have little incentive to use it wisely.

THE CASE OF BANGLADESH

As mentioned above, Japanese foreign aid was a major factor in the emergence of newly industrialising economies in Thailand and other Southeast Asian countries during the 1980s and 1990s. Tokyo's ODA was implemented in tandem with extensive Japanese private investment and profitable joint ventures with local entrepreneurs. This was not the case in Burma during 1962–1988, making it arguably an unusual, if not unique, case. But the experience of Burma's western neighbour, Bangladesh, shows that Burma was not the only exception to the 'Thailand scenario'. After it achieved independence from Pakistan in 1971, this desperately poor, overpopulated country received even more grant and loan funds from Japan than Burma. Between 1980 and 1988, total ODA disbursed to Bangladesh was US$1.85 billion, or 30 percent more than the Burmese total in the same period of US$1.42 billion (see Table 3.2 on p. 67).

According to Yanagihara Toru, large scale Japanese aid to Bangladesh was motivated by two factors: (1) its geographical location in South Asia, a 'new frontier for Japanese ODA' following the economic success stories of East and Southeast Asian countries, which had less need for aid; and (2) the perception of the Japanese government that it had to play a more active role in international efforts to alleviate poverty in the Least Developed Countries, of which Bangladesh is the largest in terms of population. Although support for humanitarian aid inside the Japanese aid establishment has never been particularly strong, Yanagihara interprets the generosity of aid to Dhaka in terms of the goal of 'cultivation of goodwill toward Japan within the international community'.[54]

As in Burma, project and non-project (commodity) loans predominated during the late 1970s and 1980s. Major projects were in energy and manufacturing, including electric power generating and fertilizer facilities. However, unlike the case of Burma, there was no Bangladesh lobby among Japanese politicians, bureaucrats, private business or ordinary citizens.[55] Although Japanese and British forces fought bitter battles across the Naaf River in Arakan (now Burma's Arakan State) during World War II, Japan's historical connection with Bangladesh or its predecessors (East Pakistan before 1971, British-ruled Bengal before Partition in 1947) had been minimal. There is no Bangladeshi equivalent to *Harp of Burma, biru-kichi,* or (initially, at least) personal networks linking influential people inside Japanese and Bangladeshi society. Japanese and Bangladeshis, most of whom are Muslim, do not share a common religion. Unlike Burma, the country does not have rich natural resources that would figure in Tokyo's economic survivalist strategies.

Apart from the reasons given by Yanagihara, a convincing argument can be made that generous aid to Bangladesh is another example of the 'boomerang economy' at work. This suggests that shared history and personal connections, which people argue have made Burma a special case, may have played a less important role in the generosity of Tokyo's ODA than is commonly assumed. In other words, Burma, like Bangladesh, was a suitable locale for the building of expensive loan projects that brought revenues to powerful domestic constituencies inside Japan, and perhaps less than optimal benefit to the recipient country.

BURMA IN JAPAN'S ECONOMIC STRATEGIES: THE ILLUSION OF REFORM

Profits from the 'boomerang economy' aside, Burma was well situated within the regional focus of Japanese economic cooperation programs after World War II. The loss of China markets after the People's Republic was established in 1949 and the payment of reparations not only to Burma but to Indonesia, the Philippines and South Vietnam opened the Southeast Asia region to Japanese capital at a time when the United States, then (as now) Japan's most important ally, was encouraging Japanese trade and investment in order to promote the stability of non-communist regimes. Japan promoted a cooperative 'heart-to-heart' relationship with the Association of South East Asian Nations (ASEAN) during the prime ministership of Fukuda Takeo (1976–1978), who committed his government to doubling the amount of money allocated to aid programs.[56] The chief beneficiaries were the ASEAN countries, but Burma received more than a few crumbs from the newly groaning table of Japanese ODA. Although a socialist state like China or Vietnam, Ne Win's regime, practising a foreign policy of strict non-alignment, never found itself the object of a Washington-led economic quarantine, which Japan would probably have been obliged to join.

The Japanese have traditionally viewed Burma as a country with great economic potential. As mentioned in Chapter One, it was one of the wealthiest countries in Asia before World War II, a major producer of petroleum and the world's largest exporter of rice. With low population to land ratios compared to other Southeast Asian nations, its agricultural potential is huge. There are large natural gas fields offshore, and the country also has significant deposits of minerals such as tin, silver, and tungsten, not to mention rubies and jade. It has the world's largest (though rapidly diminishing) teak forests, other tropical woods, and offshore fisheries. Altogether, Burma is a treasure house of natural resources surpassed in Southeast Asia only by Indonesia.

The people's literacy rate is high. Thanks largely to Ne Win-era policies that depressed standards of living for almost three decades after 1962, Burmese labour was, and remains today, extremely cheap. The country's per capita G.N.P. was only US$200 in 1991, compared to US$490 for Indonesia and US$1,160 for Thailand.[57] Its strategic location at the juncture of Southeast, East and South Asia makes it potentially ideal for the export of natural resources and cheap manufactured goods to those regions.

Japanese general trading companies (*sōgō shōsha*) continued to maintain offices in Rangoon during the 1962–1988 socialist era. Two were operating during the initial period of nationalizations in the 1960s. By the late 1980s, their number had grown to 11.[58] The size of ODA ensured them a role in procurement for aid projects. But they were also in an excellent position to benefit from an improvement in the economic climate. Yet their presence is remarkable given the near-total lack of other foreign private firms in Burma.[59]

During the 1970s, the Ne Win regime modified its previously rigid socialist policies and won the financial support of major aid donors. Inflation, shortages of vital goods, social unrest and an attempted coup d'état by young officers in July 1976 threatened the regime's survival. In late 1976, Ne Win asked for as much as US$2 billion in foreign aid for development projects.[60] The World Bank established an Aid Burma Consultative Group (also known as the Burma Aid Group) consisting of ten donor nations and multilateral lenders to map plans for Burma's economic development. It held its first meeting, at Japan's invitation, in Tokyo in November 1976. Burma's record as a responsible debtor in the past and the apparent sincerity of its reform programme were major factors in the increase in ODA from all donors in the late 1970s.[61]

In the early 1980s, the limited liberalization encouraged by the Burma Aid Group seemed promising. GNP growth, averaging 5.95 percent between 1976 and 1984, was comparable to that of neighbouring countries.[62] The most dynamic sector at the time was agriculture, due to the introduction of high yield varieties of rice. Japanese aid in the form of fertilizers and pesticides also played a role in impressive increases in rice harvests reported in official Burmese government statistics.[63]

The volume of Japanese aid expanded rapidly at this time. According to statistics published by the Ministry of International Trade and Industry (MITI), grant and loan aid commitments increased almost 450 per cent between the 1976 and 1977 Japanese fiscal years (begins 1 April).[64] Disbursements from Tokyo increased more than 500 per cent, from US$20.6 million in 1977 to US$104 million in 1978.[65] Japanese policymakers, operating in an environment in which ODA programs as a whole were rapidly expanding, responded to what seemed to be a changing economic environment. Aid allocations by other major donors, including West Germany, also increased. But Ne Win's strategies and the Burma Aid Group's attempts to encourage liberalization ultimately failed. By the late 1980s, the realization of Burma's economic potential seemed more remote than ever.

Even before the 18 September 1988 seizure of power by the State Law and Order Restoration Council, Japanese policymakers were beginning to have second thoughts about the country's economic direction. There were no new allocations for loan projects after 1986, although grant funding and technical assistance continued on a limited basis.[66] As mentioned above, commodity loans for the four industrial projects were halted in 1987, after a study revealed their inefficiency and continued dependence on Japanese-made rather than locally-made components.[67] Still more serious was the country's debt crisis. Previously a careful borrower, Burma had piled up an external debt – which consisted mostly of concessional loans from Japan and West Germany – of around US$5 billion. As the yen and deutschmark appreciated and revenues from traditional raw materials exports such as rice, lentils and teak declined during the mid- and late 1980s, the government could not meet rapidly mounting debt service obligations.[68]

In early 1988, Aung Gyi, Ne Win's fellow general who had led the quasi-reparations negotiations and had been forced off the Revolutionary Council in 1963, met with Japanese businessmen and politicians in Rangoon. They expressed to him Tokyo's frustration over the lack of progress in economic reform. In one of a series of widely publicised letters to Ne Win, Aung Gyi wrote that 'Though Japan has provided economic and technical assistance to Burma for many years, there has been no ... success in any sector.' He concluded that 'Japan no longer has any faith in the present ... regime and has decided to cut down on the assistance ... unless you [Ne Win] change the whole team.'[69]

In April 1988, Burma's deputy prime minister, U Tun Tin, visited Tokyo to ask for debt relief and more economic assistance. In meetings with the Japanese prime minister and finance minister, he was advised of the desirability of undertaking certain unspecified economic reforms. They also suggested that a discussion of reforms might occur within the context of a meeting of Burma's major aid donors, including multilateral agencies such as the World Bank and the Asian Development Bank. The Burma Aid Group had become largely inactive during the 1980s because Ne Win preferred bilateral negotiations with individual donor countries.[70] Such recommendations on Japan's part were natural since Burma had acquired Least Developed Country status from the United Nations in December 1987. But they may also have been a response to Ne Win's arbitrary decision to demonetize Burma's bank notes without compensation in September 1987. This ill-considered policy, designed to curb the black market (what the government called 'economic insurgency'), caused a great deal of hardship among ordinary people and sparked student demonstrations, the first since the mid-1970s. Some observers believe that the Japanese government was considering a major change in aid policy even before the political crisis of summer and fall 1988.[71]

ODA AS NE WIN'S LIFE RAFT

Although Burma is a Buddhist country, popular beliefs about the supernatural abound. Usually, these beliefs coexist rather than conflict with Buddhism. The gilded, 99-meter high Shwe Dagon Pagoda in Rangoon, Burma's most sacred Buddhist site where the relics of four Buddhas are believed to be preserved, contains shrines to the eight planets whose movements are said to influence the lives of men. People make offerings at the planetary post corresponding to the day on which they were born.[72] In traditional Burmese society, it was customary to keep a horoscope composed by a professional astrologer, and consult it on important occasions, a practice that continues today. Many of the top members of the present ruling junta, the State Peace and Development Council, have personal astrologers.[73] Throughout his life, Ne Win was also a fervent believer in astrology. Across from the Shwe Dagon is a second, smaller pagoda, the Maha Vizaya ('Great Victory'), the construction of which was sponsored by Burma's leader during the 1980s. Unlike most pagodas, it is hollow, and the ceiling of the central chamber is decorated with astrological symbols.

Not far from the Shwe Dagon and Maha Wizaya pagodas is a planetarium that was built with Japanese grant aid, part of a project designed to promote science education, completed in 1986. According to journalist Bertil Lintner, writing in *AERA*, a Japanese weekly magazine, the planetarium's chief purpose was not to educate students about astronomy but to further Ne Win's astrological investigations. Closed to the general public, the electric-powered planetarium could be used to plot the stars and planets for any date, and was consulted by Burma's leader whenever important political decisions had to be made.[74] If true (a Burma specialist with the Japanese foreign ministry dismissed Lintner's allegations as an 'overly cynical view'), this is probably the most unusual application of the principle of *yōsei shugi* ('request-ism') in the history of Japan's official development assistance!

The Burma–Japan relationship during 1962–1988, especially the ODA connection, must be understood in terms of not only domestic constituencies and regional strategies on the part of the donor, but also the special characteristics of the government of the recipient nation. Although this has been discussed to some extent above, a closer examination of the BSPP regime reveals a paradox: its policies of centralised state planning and isolation impoverished the nation; but in the twilight years of Burmese socialism, ODA became increasingly necessary for its survival, until the whole system came crashing down in 1988. In other words, ODA from capitalist nations became a life raft for a failed socialist state.

Ne Win's enforcement of a rigid, Eastern European style socialist economic system and strict non-alignment in foreign relations, amounting to isolationism, reflected his determination to eliminate foreign influences not only in the economic but also in the social and cultural spheres. Educational exchanges with foreign countries were cut off, and after 1962 few Burmese scholars studied abroad. English was de-emphasized in favour of Burmese in school curricula, and foreign missionary schools, among Burma's best, were nationalized, and their foreign teachers sent home. Ne Win's apologists often describe this isolationism as a reaction against the alienation and oppression of the colonial era, when, as described in Chapter One, foreigners controlled the modern economy and exploited indigenous peoples, especially the Burmans. According to Michael Aung-Thwin, in an oft-quoted essay on Burma's 'myth of independence', the Ne Win regime represented a return to authentic and historically-sanctioned Burmese (or Burman) values after decades of imposed westernisation.[75]

As mentioned in Chapter One, Burma's multi-ethnic, plural society had already been substantially undermined in the early months of World War II, when hundreds of thousands of South Asians fled the country for British India. But during the parliamentary era (1948–1962), Indian, Pakistani and Chinese business classes remained economically important. Ne Win uprooted them through a confiscatory demonetization measure in 1964 and a wave of nationalizations, causing 196,000 South Asians to leave the country by 1972.[76] Following bloody anti-Chinese riots in 1967, many members of this minority also left the country. The demise of Burma's economically dynamic if culturally ambiguous plural society was reflected in population figures for the capital city. In 1931, Rangoon's population was 67 per cent foreign (including Hindu and Muslim South Asians, Chinese, Europeans, Anglo-Burmese, Anglo-Indians, Jews and Armenians); by 1983, foreigners (defined as 'associate citizens' of non-indigenous ancestry as well as much smaller numbers of foreign passport holders) comprised only 7.4 per cent of city residents.[77] As late as 1960, Rangoon was still one of Asia's most modern cities; ten years later, it was a decaying if picturesque ruin.

The 'Burmanization' of the economy and its control through state owned and state managed corporations had disastrous consequences, on both a large and small scale. Because the state enforced artificially low prices for rice and other agricultural goods and the distribution system was inefficient and corrupt, Burmese people, whose country had been a major exporter of rice even after World War II, suffered serious food shortages for the first time in their history during the 1960s and 1970s, leading to recurrent social unrest. Most farmers preferred to avoid state procurers and sell their rice on the more profitable black market, creating scarcities at the best of times and catastrophe when drought or floods made for poor harvests. Nationalized factories, managed by inexperienced military officers, could not produce consumer necessities in sufficient quantities, and people could not obtain them through the official network of People's Stores and Cooperatives. Much of the government's budget was spent on fighting insurgents, especially the Burma Communist Party based along the China–Burma border, meaning that spending on health, education and infrastructure was minimal. The banking system was a shambles and fears of demonetization pervasive. Those who could afford it kept their wealth in gold or gemstones, while Burmese merchant seamen (who usually got their jobs through the right connections) made small fortunes importing second-hand Japanese vehicles.

University students faced bleak prospects after graduation (many became pedicab drivers) and repeatedly protested against the regime in the mid-1970s, most notably during the bloody U Thant Incident of December 1974, when they captured the coffin containing the remains of the U.N. Secretary General and brought it to the Rangoon University campus.[78] Even the military élite was affected by the economic rot. In July 1976, an officers' plot to assassinate Ne Win, San Yu and Tin Oo, the increasingly powerful director of Military Intelligence, was exposed; the fourteen young captains and majors involved wanted an end to the socialist system, the acceptance of foreign private investment and possibly a new government led by the purged defence minister Tin U. It seemed that shortages of necessities caused hardship for the *Tatmadaw* rank-and-file, despite the army's privileged economic position.

The regime's continued survival increasingly depended upon connections with 'economic insurgents' (black market entrepreneurs), often working in cooperation with border area insurgents. They provided consumers with a high-priced alternative to the official economy, a kind of economic safety valve. Kyaw Yin Hlaing writes that BSPP and state officials, who could not rely on government budgets to provide them with the funds needed for their official duties, typically obtained cash and goods from the black marketeers, offering them protection in return in fluid patron-client relationships. In addition, these officials, many of whom were military officers, made substantial profits from siphoning goods out of the official economy, where they had privileged access, to the black market. The underground economy had become so entrenched that when Ne Win ordered his sudden demonetization measure without compensation in September 1987, hitting hard at the entrepreneurs and all who were dependent upon them, the economy went into a tailspin, causing widespread hardship that was arguably the major factor in the eruption of massive anti-government protests the following year.[79]

At a 1981 BSPP congress, Ne Win warned that 'Foreign governments … use their aid to exploit well-meaning but inexperienced nations.'[80] But like the 'economic insurgents', donors of ODA gave his regime an economic prop that could not be obtained through other means. Had such aid not been available, the BSPP regime might have collapsed even before 1988.[81]

Japan was, compared to other donor countries, a trustable and non-threatening source of funds. The *yōsei shugi* principle meant that expensive projects could be built without Ne Win having to modify economic policies to fit comprehensive development strategies, even if the projects were not effectively utilised after completion. Moreover, Japan after 1945 was not a military power. Unlike the United States and China, both of which had interfered on a large scale in Burma's internal affairs after independence in 1948, Japan posed no security threat.[82] Loan and grant funds for aid projects made it possible to allocate scarce government funds for more pressing priorities, such as fighting insurgents. The projects also made for good display value at a time when the regime could claim few successes.

The symbiotic relationship between the Japanese and Burmese polities – one an affluent promoter of a 'boomerang economy', the other a failed socialist state desperately in need of capital –

continued despite the economic reversals of the mid-1980s. But 1988, when nationwide protests broke out and the socialist system suddenly collapsed, was a crucial turning point.

NOTES

[1] Price (2001).

[2] Indonesia signed but did not ratify the treaty, while under heavy pressure from the U.S. the Philippines ratified it, but belatedly. Vietnam, Laos and Cambodia signed, but Indochina was still ruled by the French colonial regime, which at the time was fighting the Viet Minh-led movement for independence. Ibid.

[3] *Myanmā Nyūsu* [Myanmar News] (1991: 20).

[4] *Far Eastern Economic Review* (1955); Walinsky (1962: 169).

[5] *Far Eastern Economic Review* (1960).

[6] Walinsky (1962: 512, 513); Steinberg (1990: 55, 56).

[7] Söderberg (1996: 33).

[8] *Far Eastern Economic Review* (1960).

[9] Steinberg (1990: 61).

[10] Kudo (1994: 3, 4); Olson (1961: 3–9); Steinberg (1990: 61; 2001: 255) says that a concessional loan of US$60 million was included along with the US$140 million quasi-reparations agreement in 1963.

[11] Comment of retired Japanese diplomat to author, Tokyo, August 1991; comment of Asian diplomat to author, Kyoto, March 1996.

[12] Walinsky (1962: 513).

[13] Steinberg (1990a: 15).

[14] Olson (1961: 1, 2).

[15] Ibid., 3.

[16] Ibid., 3–5, 12; Union of Burma (1960: 266–71).

[17] Kudo (1994: 3).

[18] Mainichi Shimbun Sha (1990: 8–12).

[19] Ibid; and Interview of Japanese Burma expert with author, Tokyo, February 1992.

20 Seekins (1992: 249).

21 OECD (1969–1975, 1971–1977, 1976–1979, 1978–1981, 1979–1982, 1980–1983, 1981–1984, 1983–1986, 1984–1987, 1985–1988: s.v., 'Burma').

22 Japan. Ministry of Foreign Affairs (1987–1990: table 7); Rudner (1989: 92).

23 JICA (1988: 20); Orr (1990: 70).

24 Institute of Developing Economies (1983: 32, 33).

25 OECD (1973–79/1985–88: s.v. 'Burma').

26 Japan. Ministry of Foreign Affairs (1987–90: table 7); Rudner (1989: 92).

27 Hadley (1990: 51, 52).

28 Pranee (1990: 51–76); Suthy (1990: 77–109); Kosai and Matsuyama (1991: 72).

29 The consortium, which included the Japan National Oil Corporation and 11 private firms, established a joint venture with the Myanma Oil Corporation with an initial investment of ¥139 million. In February 1983, a test boring yielded 1.1 cubic meters/day of natural gas from what would later be known as the Yadana field. See *Ajia-Chū-Tō Dōkō Nempō* (1982: 411), *Tōnan Ajia Yōran* (1982: 9–13), Wickman (1983: 165).

30 Zöllner (1994: 197–203).

31 Orr (1990: 59).

32 Ibid., 23, 85.

33 Comments of present and retired officials, Japanese Ministry of Foreign Affairs, to author, Tokyo, February and August 1991.

34 Steinberg (1990: 52); Mainichi Shimbun (1990: 7–22).

35 Saitō (1989: 61–63).

36 Ibid., 62, 63; Saitō (1992: 17–27).

37 JICA (1988: 19–38).

38 Ibid..

39 According to Steinberg (1990: 56), leaders in Shan State before the 1962 coup d'état expressed discontent over the small amount of development funds reaching the ethnic minority regions, including reparations.

40 Nihon–Biruma Kyōkai [Nihon–Myanmar Kyokai] (1989); Saitō (1992: 22, 23).

41 Ibid.; Sayre (1989: 7, 8).

42 Ishigaki (1988: 77).

43 Nihon–Biruma Kyōkai (1989).

44 Kakazu (1991: 24).

45 Orr (1990: 19–51).

46 Söderberg (1996: 47).

47 Ibid., 53–56; Orr (1990: 28, 59).

48 Orr (1990: 24).

49 Mainichi Shimbun Sha (1990: 28); comment of official, Japan Ministry of Foreign Affairs, to author, Tokyo, February 1991.

50 During the 1990s, China provided the *Tatmadaw*, the Burmese armed forces, with military trucks, but these models were not as sturdy or reliable as the old Hinos.

51 Orr (1990: 60); Söderberg (1996: 78, 79).

52 Ibid., 60–63; Rix (1989–90: 464).

53 Mainichi Shimbun Sha (1990: 162).

54 Yanagihara (1993: 189, 190).

55 Ibid., 190.

56 Orr (1990: 110, 111); Söderberg (1996: 35, 92).

57 Asian Development Bank (1991: 278, table A2).

58 Saitō (1989a: 7, 8). The eleven trading companies were: Sumitomo Shōji, Mitsui Bussan, Mitsubishi Shōji, Nichimen, Marubeni, Nisshō Iwai, C. Itoh, Kinshō Mataichi, Tōmen, Kanematsu Gōshō, and Daimaru.

59 See Söderberg on *sōgō shōsha* (1996: 79–87).

60 Martin (1977: 157).

61 Trager and Scully (1978: 143–45).

62 International Monetary Fund (1990: 522–25).

63 Comment of Burma analyst, Institute of Developing Economies, to author, Tokyo, February 1991.

64 MITI (1978: 428).

65 OECD (1973–79: s.v. 'Burma').

66 Japan Ministry of Foreign Affairs (1991: 132, 133); Holloway (1988: 10, 11).

67 Mainchi Shimbun Sha (1990: 12, 13); comment of Japanese Burma specialist to author, Tokyo, February 1992.

68 Asian Development Bank (1991: 146–48).

69 Lintner (1988: 18); Holloway (1988: 10, 11).

70 Comment of official, Japanese Ministry of Foreign Affairs, to author, Tokyo, June 1991.

71 Steinberg (1990: 67).

72 The traditional Burmese week has eight days, two of which are included in Wednesday.

73 Aung Zaw (2003: 27).

74 Lintner (1992: 26).

75 Aung Thwin (1989: 19–34).

76 Kyaw Yin Hlaing (2003: 13).

77 Mya Than and Ananda Rajah (1996: 239, table 8.5).

78 Selth (1989: 1–31). Troops went on the campus and recaptured it on 11 December, killing possibly hundreds of students.

79 Kyaw Yin Hlaing (2003: 53–57).

80 Silverstein (1982: 188).

81 Steinberg (2001: 256).

82 The United States supported Kuomintang military activity along the Burma-China border in the 1950s; after the 1967 anti-Chinese riots, Beijing supported the Burma Communist Party's North-eastern Command along the same border.

Chapter Four

JAPAN'S RESPONSES TO THE POST-1988 POLITICAL CRISIS IN BURMA

Like World War II, the events of 1988 brought revolutionary changes to Burma. The year witnessed a nationwide popular uprising against the Ne Win regime, his retirement as chairman of the Burma Socialist Programme Party after 26 years in power, the demise of the 'Burmese Road to Socialism', and the violent re-imposition of military rule under a new junta, the State Law and Order Restoration Council (SLORC).

The intensity of popular opposition to the Ne Win regime in 1988 was unexpected, not only by foreign diplomats in Rangoon, but by Ne Win himself, who after the first clashes between university students and Riot Police occurred in March, took his customary vacation in Europe the following month, returning in late May.[1] The crisis began as the escalation of a small incident, fed by government incompetence and heavy-handedness. On the night of 12 March 1988, a fight broke out between students of the Rangoon Institute of Technology (RIT) and local youths at a teashop near the RIT campus, which resulted in a student being injured by a local and the latter being arrested. On the following day, RIT students learned that the local youth had been released because his father was a member of the People's Council (an organ of local government under the BSPP) and held a protest.

Had the protest been handled with restraint by the authorities, it might have been forgotten. But units of the Riot Police (*Lon Htein*) assaulted demonstrators with deadly force, killing at least three students and wounding many others. Over the next few days, the authorities suppressed further student protests with incomprehensible brutality. The worst of these early incidents occurred on 16 March at the White Bridge, an embankment on the western shore of Inya Lake in northern Rangoon where university students marching from downtown to RIT were trapped between detachments of the *Tatmadaw* and Riot Police. According to an 8 June letter written by retired Brigadier Aung Gyi to Ne Win, almost three hundred students were killed, including those whom the police drowned in the lake.[2]

On 21 June, Riot Police again attacked students during a protest march near the Myeinigone Market, located northwest of the Shwe Dagon Pagoda. This incident was significant because not only students but the general public took part, neighbourhood residents giving students refuge and even fighting alongside them against the police with primitive weapons, a precursor to the massive public demonstrations of 'Democracy Summer'.[3] After student activists declared a general strike on 8 August 1988 (known as the 'Four Eights Movement'), huge demonstrations occurred in Rangoon and other cities, and the *Tatmadaw*, having imposed martial law, shot at citizens point-blank, killing hundreds. More killings occurred in the wake of the 18 September seizure of power by the SLORC, when the army systematically 'pacified' Burma's cities.

These violent events occurred against a background of shortages of rice and other necessities, fuelling inflation and a pervasive atmosphere of distress. Food shortages had occurred before, in the late 1960s and the mid-1970s, and there had been popular unrest – especially in 1974, when the country was crippled by widespread labour strikes and students held their memorial service on the Rangoon University campus for deceased United Nations Secretary General U Thant, which ended in a bloody crackdown by the army.[4]

But Ne Win's September 1987 demonetization decree, which rendered as much as sixty to eighty percent of all *kyat* currency notes suddenly worthless without compensation, was one of the most important factors in 1988's popular outrage.[5] This measure, designed to cripple 'economic insurgency' (the black market), caused hardship for rich and poor alike, since most people kept their savings in cash rather than in the unreliable state banking system. When mass demonstrations broke out in summer of the following year, the first to participate, apart from the student activists, were day-labourers and trishaw-men, who had been deprived of employment by the demonetization.[6] Working class districts of Rangoon – especially the satellite towns of Thaketa and North and South Okkalapa – became battlefields between local residents and the army.

Popular indignation was deeply felt, but inchoate. Hatred of the regime unified the people of Rangoon and other central Burma cities: not only students and labourers, but civil servants, small business people and Buddhist monks, the latter being the most highly respected members of Burmese society. Even small numbers of armed forces personnel marched in the demonstrations of August and September, which drew hundreds of thousands of participants.

The explosion of popular rage was sustained not only by economic hardship and the regime's killing of unarmed demonstrators, but also by the government's attempts to cover up the facts concerning these events, and Ne Win's arrogance, expressed in a threat he made at the 23 July BSPP Extraordinary Congress: 'If the army shoots, it hits – there is no firing into the air to scare.'[7] Ne Win also chose Sein Lwin, the 'Butcher of Rangoon' who as commander of the *Lon Htein* had been responsible for the March and June killings, as his successor as BSPP chairman and president of the country. Popular hatred of the once-honoured *Tatmadaw* swelled in the wake of violent incidents, especially the army's 10 August attack on Rangoon General Hospital, where staff members had been holding a demonstration calling for an end to the shootings.[8]

Students established many activist groups, of which the All Burma Federation of Student Unions led by Min Ko Naing was the most prominent; but the movement was fragmented (despite regime accusations, underground 'cells' of the Communist Party of Burma based on the China–Burma border did not play an important role).

Moreover, Rangoon, the chief battleground in the stand-off between state and society, had descended into a state of anarchy by late August. City neighbourhoods elected their own committees of prominent local citizens and Buddhist monks, and blockaded themselves off from other neighbourhoods amidst an atmosphere of fear and suspicion, created in large part by regime *agents provocateurs* who committed crimes, including the poisoning of public water jars.[9] Thus, the army could move in on 18 September and break the back of the resistance with comparative ease.

With the SLORC's inception on 18 September, socialist isolationism (which, given the large infusions of ODA from Japan and other countries during the late 1970s and 1980s, was more apparent than real) broke down, and the new regime (renamed the State Peace and Development Council, or SPDC, in 1997) opened the country's chronically undeveloped economy to foreign exploitation. In words if not deeds, it committed itself to economic liberalization and free markets, following in the footsteps of China and Vietnam, where the coupling of an authoritarian state and a liberalizing economy had achieved great economic successes. Relations with Burma's Asian neighbours – China, Thailand, India and Bangladesh – were substantially improved, though the outflow of refugees and narcotics from Burma's border areas became serious problems.

The regime signed cease-fires with most of the country's insurgent groups, beginning with ethnic components of the defunct Communist Party of Burma in 1989. This brought peace to many ethnic minority areas for the first time in decades (though as of 2005, the struggle of the Karens against the central government, which began during World War II, continues). Burma became a member of the Association of South East Asian Nations (ASEAN) in 1997, an important step in its integration into the region. The country has also become a participant in such regional integration schemes as the Greater Mekong Sub-region and the Asian Highway, the latter designed to link East, Southeast and South Asia with the Middle East.

Thus, by the early years of the twenty-first century, the SPDC could claim some accomplishments. But it was unable or unwilling to tackle fundamental problems: widening gaps between rich and poor, the worsening problem of food shortages, one of Asia's worst AIDS epidemics, and deterioration of the country's health and educational systems. Like its BSPP predecessor, it has failed to achieve sustained economic growth, due in part to western economic sanctions, but principally because of the *ad hoc*, top-down nature of SPDC economic measures (which resemble the command economy of the old socialist state), a confusing system of dual (or multiple) dollar-*kyat* exchange rates, and the prevalence of economically irrational 'crony capitalism'. In business as well as other spheres of life, there was no rule of law, only patron-client networks focused on the military elite. The junta spent scarce resources building Buddhist pagodas (to acquire legitimacy among the Burmese Buddhist majority), expanding the manpower of the *Tatmadaw* (from 186,000 in 1988 to over 400,000 in the mid-1990s) and acquiring expensive weapons from abroad, such as Chinese warships, Ukrainian tanks and Russian Mig-29 fighter jets.

The SPDC remains a 'hard' authoritarian state, always on guard for a recurrence of 1988. There are over 1,500 political prisoners in Burma's jails. The government has refused to recognise the results of the 27 May 1990 general election, in which the National League for Democracy, Aung San Suu Kyi's party, won a landslide victory. Despite international encouragement, no progress has been made in carrying out dialogue between the government and the opposition leader. Most observers believe that the regime-sponsored National Convention, convened during 1993–1996 and again in 2004–2005 to draft a new constitution, is little more than a carefully policed façade to put the 1990 election issue to rest and ensure continued military domination of the political system. The SPDC's vision for the future is inspired by President Suharto's New Order in Indonesia – where the doctrine of *dwi fungsi* (Indonesian: 'dual functions') gave the military a formal role in national political life – though that system was discredited in Suharto's own country after he was ousted from power in May 1998.[10]

Given the business-oriented and economic nature of Japan's ties with Burma before 1988, it would not have been surprising if Tokyo had pursued total economic engagement with post-socialist Rangoon, much as it did with the reformist communist regime in Hanoi after it adopted *Doi Moi* (restructuring) policies in 1986. But relations with the 'friendliest country toward Japan in Asia' were complicated by new developments: international outrage over the SLORC's human rights violations and disregard of the 1990 election, which Japan could not ignore; the popularity of Aung San Suu Kyi, who even before being awarded the Nobel Peace Prize in 1991 had become a figure of international stature; and the emergence of the People's Republic of China as the country with predominant influence in post-1988 Burma, arguably at Japan's expense.

An official of Japan's Ministry of Foreign Affairs, speaking at an NGO colloquium in Tokyo in 2001, placed countries in three categories according to their response to the political crisis in Burma. The first, consisting of the United States and European Union, 'refuse to compromise human rights, democracy, and such fundamental ideals... And for this reason, their position has been to impose sanctions on Myanmar [Burma].' The second group, countries belonging to ASEAN, 'take a position of non-interference in each others' internal affairs in regard to democracy and human rights... They consider it most realistic to promote democratization in Myanmar through expanding economic contacts and being actively involved in this way.'[11]

The third category, which includes Japan (and Australia), takes:

> ... a position which places importance on human rights and democracy as a matter of course, but on the other hand, together with our fellow Asian countries, we prefer not to use sanctions, but to speak as friends. What are the expectations of the international community? What needs to be done for Myanmar to be accepted into the international community? These are things we are in a position to discuss quietly.[12]

The evolution of this middle road between the West and ASEAN, which Japanese diplomats frequently described as a policy of 'quiet dialogue' (*shizuka na taiwa*) or a 'sunshine policy' (*taiyō seisaku*), brought into play a number of constituencies both inside and outside the Japanese political system who fashioned a complex and often ambiguous response to Burma's failure to achieve political reconciliation and economic development after 1988, as will be discussed in Chapter Five.

CRITICAL DISTANCE: AUGUST 1988–FEBRUARY 1989

On the numerically auspicious day of 8 August 1988 (the 'Four Eights'), activist students led massive demonstrations and a general strike to drive the universally-hated Sein Lwin from office as president, a goal achieved with his resignation four days later. At the time, there were about 280 Japanese residents in Burma, most of whom – diplomats, employees of trading companies, aid officials and their families – lived in Rangoon. The strikes and demonstrations continued into September as people demanded the resignation of Sein Lwin's successor, Dr. Maung Maung, and establishment of an interim government. For reasons of safety, the Ministry of Foreign Affairs in Tokyo warned Japanese nationals not to visit the country and urged those in Burma to leave.[13]

On 13 September, just five days before the SLORC seizure of power, the Japanese government announced a freeze on ODA disbursements due to unsettled conditions.[14] On 19 September, a Ministry of Foreign Affairs spokesman expressed concern for the worsening political situation and the hope that political stability would be restored and promises of economic reform fulfilled. The import of this and other official statements was that ODA flows would not be reopened until there was substantial improvement on both the political and economic fronts.[15] On 28 September, Ohtaka Hiroshi, Japan's ambassador in Rangoon, expressed hope that further bloodshed would be avoided and that there would be a 'peaceful, democratic resolution of the crisis in accordance with the general wishes of the people.'[16] He also conveyed the Japanese government's understanding that the new martial law regime was provisional rather than permanent in nature and urged it to begin dialogue with the opposition, reiterating the position that restarting ODA was conditional upon political stabilization and genuine economic reform. He also stated that expression of these views, made to U Ohn Gyaw, a senior official in the Burmese foreign ministry who later became foreign minister, did not constitute recognition of the SLORC by the Japanese government.[17] The speed and apparent determination with which Japan joined western countries in condemning the SLORC was a source of surprise to many observers.[18]

Ambassador Ohtaka played a decisive role in Tokyo's initial policy of 'critical distance'. A career diplomat, he and his wife, Ohtaka Yoshiko (who was chairperson of the Nihon–Biruma Kyōkai), had been close friends of Ne Win for many years. On an earlier posting to Rangoon, Mrs. Ohtaka had become acquainted with Ne Win's wife, Kitty Ba Than, and the two couples frequently dined together. Even after Kitty Ba Than died in 1974, the Ohtakas enjoyed Ne Win's confidence. But the events of 1988 caused the ambassador to end his friendship with the old dictator.[19]

The government's brutality against its own citizens disgusted him, and he was sceptical about SLORC chairman General Saw Maung's promise to transfer power to a civilian government after holding a general election. On 4 January 1989, Ohtaka joined the ambassadors of western countries in boycotting the new regime's Independence Day celebrations.[20] The boycott enraged SLORC, which railed against 'those intellectuals in developed countries who despise Asians, including Burmese. This pitiful clique [of ambassadors] is an example. Although the Burmese government and people treat guests with great care, they shouldn't be crafty or insulting.'[21]

Relations between the junta and Ohtaka were further strained because the generals believed that he was responsible for the Japanese government's decision to suspend aid, which was reaffirmed on 13 January 1989 when it cancelled grants worth yen 927.0 million (US$7.3 million).[22] At the time, SLORC was desperately short of cash. The economy was in chaos and hard currency reserves were seriously depleted. The junta needed funds to give its officers and men substantial pay increases, in order to buy their loyalty at a time when the danger of a split in the *Tatmadaw* and a 'Fidel Ramos scenario' (referring to the top general who broke with Ferdinand Marcos and supported the People's Power Revolution in the Philippines in February 1986) seemed imminent.

While Ambassador Ohtaka took the side of the Burmese people against their rulers, influential circles in Tokyo had a different perspective. Some indication of the direction the policy debate on Burma was taking is found in a December 1988 article published in *Gaikō Foramu* (*Diplomacy Forum*), a monthly magazine that expresses the views of the foreign policy establishment. Titled 'Enjo taikoku e no jōken' ('Conditions for Japan to become an ODA great power'), it consisted of a round-table discussion between an official of the Economic Cooperation Bureau of the Ministry of Foreign Affairs, the chairman of the Marubeni Trading Company, and an academic economist. Alluding to a television interview in which Aung San Suu Kyi had criticized the Japanese government for giving a great deal of aid to the Burmese government but not showing support for the pro-democracy movement, the moderator invited the participants to comment. In the economist's words,

> This is a difficult problem. I may be misinformed, but because aid is part of the diplomatic relations between countries, there is no other alternative but to work with the existing political regime. For example, there was criticism that aid to the Philippines supported the Marcos dictatorship. But there was a flood in Manila, and without pumps donated by Japanese ODA, the downtown areas of the city would have been inundated. This was an important issue no matter who the leadership was in terms of the people's livelihood and health.[23]

To which Marubeni's chairman added: 'Anti-government forces certainly cannot expect Japan to give them money. This is government-to-government aid. If, for example, Suu Kyi forms a government, and if Japan recognized it, aid perhaps would be forthcoming.'[24] Both panellists opposed the linkage of aid to *political* conditions, an issue that would loom large in Tokyo's post-1988 relations with the SLORC.

According to a U.S. State Department official interviewed by this writer, Washington placed considerable pressure on a reluctant Japanese government to freeze ODA as the crisis intensified in late 1988.[25] If this is true, it reflects another important post-1988 theme, *Myanmā masatsu* ('Myanmar friction' in Japanese) between Washington and Tokyo on their different approaches to dealing with the military regime.

BREAKING RANKS: JAPAN RECOGNIZES THE SLORC

It took almost five months for the various Japanese government agencies involved in Burma–Japan relations to agree to extend formal recognition (*shōnin* in Japanese) to the SLORC and reopen the pipeline of committed aid without allocation of funds for new projects. The decision was announced on 17 February 1989, when Ambassador Ohtaka conveyed the news to SLORC chairman General Saw Maung.[26]

The foreign reaction was largely critical. One western diplomat described the re-establishment of formal relations as 'shocking and capricious', which 'just proves you cannot trust Japan to behave responsibly'.[27] On 24 February, U.S. Senator Daniel P. Moynihan issued a statement expressing his 'gravest concerns' and his opinion that aid should not be given until the regime established genuine democracy.[28] SLORC's opponents in Burma were also unhappy. In an interview with a Thai newspaper, Aung San Suu Kyi said that 'I think it would have been so much better if people could put human rights issues above economic issues, especially in a country like Burma where the human rights issue is so pressing.'[29]

The details of the consensus-building process within the Japanese government that led to the 17 February announcement are unclear, but normalization seems to have been the result of a compromise between: (1) the Ministry of Finance, which was reluctant to allow the flow of even committed aid because Burma was billions of yen in arrears on debt payments; (2) the Ministry of Trade and Industry, which represented those business interests who had a huge stake in ODA contracts and anticipated future opportunities in light of the SLORC's economic liberalization policies; and (3) the Ministry of Foreign Affairs, which wanted to preserve the historical friendship between the two countries and at the same time had to respond to the criticism of western governments, especially the United States, which opposed the restoration of aid.

Normalization and ODA disbursement were closely linked. According to a 17 February Kyodo news service dispatch:

> Japan will provide a total of some 100 billion yen in grants and loans, which it already committed to giving, and emergency aid based on humanitarian considerations.
>
> The [foreign ministry] officials, however, said Tokyo would wait and see how matters in Burma progress before deciding whether to provide new financial assistance to the impoverished Southeast Asian country.
>
> Japan's ODA to Burma in 1986 amounted to 244 million dollars, accounting for some 80 per cent of total foreign aid to Burma in that year.[30]

The timing of recognition coincided with the SLORC's announcement, on 16 February 1989, that multi-party general elections would take place before June 1990. According to a correspondent for the *Far Eastern Economic Review*, an unofficial Japanese mission, including a MITI official, went to Rangoon in early February without the knowledge of the Japanese embassy and met with Burmese foreign ministry officials, who told them of the election timetable. Private parties inside Japan, moreover, lobbied for normalization, including corporate interests and politically influential groups of war veterans who complained that the lack of normal ties between the two countries prevented them from visiting the graves of their fallen comrades.[31] Critics inside Japan claimed that Japan's decision to recognize the SLORC was largely influenced by the 25 January 1989 petition presented to the government by the Nihon–Biruma Kyōkai. Aside from the economic costs of the aid freeze discussed in Chapter Three, the petition mentioned that without official recognition, a Burmese delegation would not be able to attend the funeral ceremony for the Shōwa Emperor (Hirohito), scheduled for 24 February 1989.[32]

Foreign ministry spokesmen denied that the petition played any part in normalization, claiming that the close timing with the 17 February announcement was coincidental. They argued, moreover, that the decision was made on strictly legalistic premises: the new regime had established effective control over the country and had not violated international laws or treaties. In addition, recognition was justified on the grounds that it would give Japan the opportunity to maintain dialogue with the SLORC to promote democratisation and economic reform. In contrast with other countries, Japan's laws require the government to decide whether or not to formally recognize any new regime that comes to power through extralegal means such as a coup d'état ('government-to-government' recognition rather than 'state-to-state' recognition). Without such a procedure, Japanese officials would not be able to maintain effective contact with their counterparts in Rangoon. Operating on a 'state to state' basis, the United States and European countries did not need to extend formal recognition.[33]

Critics, including Aung San Suu Kyi, argued that normalization and a partial reopening of the ODA pipeline was a triumph for traditional Japanese-style 'money politics' and ODA's status as a cash cow for well-connected corporations. But from the perspective of early 1989, normalisation facilitated 'quiet dialogue' between Tokyo and Rangoon, promising good results all around: an orderly transfer of power to a democratic, civilian government after the SLORC held general elections; and the benefits of economic engagement not only for Japanese businesses but also for the Burmese people, now that Ne Win-style socialism had been scrapped. The assumption was that Burma would follow the liberalizing and civil society-building trends of its Asian neighbours. This never happened – for reasons connected to Burma's distinct historical experience, the power monopoly of the *Tatmadaw* and the growing influence of China. As the SLORC years wore on, Ambassador Ohtaka's scepticism about the new regime proved correct.

HOPES FRUSTRATED: JAPAN AND THE 27 MAY 1990 ELECTION

The general election of 27 May 1990 was a unique event in modern Burmese history, drawing the hitherto little-known country into the international spotlight. Other authoritarian states such as China and Vietnam have never held multi-party elections, and have continued – despite occasional international criticism of their human rights records – to receive large amounts of foreign aid and private investment from Japan and other countries. But as mentioned, the SLORC's experiment with representative government backfired badly: the main opposition party, Aung San Suu Kyi's National League for Democracy (NLD), won a landslide victory (392 seats out of 485 contested, and 59.9 per cent of the popular vote). When the junta refused to transfer power to the elected government, as Saw Maung had originally promised, his regime became an international pariah, the target of criticism and sanctions by western governments and a global network of activists, including newly exiled Burmese students, who wanted to make the country the 'South Africa of the 1990s'.[34]

The SLORC's election strategy was driven by complex and often obscure motives. At the July 1988 emergency congress of the Burma Socialist Programme Party (which transformed itself into a 'democratic' party, the National Unity Party [NUP], after the 18 September coup), Ne Win proposed a popular referendum on whether the socialist-era single party system should be scrapped in favour of a multi-party system. Though his proposal was rejected, his successor Dr. Maung Maung committed himself to holding multi-party elections. A redundantly named Elections Commission for Holding Democratic Multi-Party General Elections was established and was one of the few institutions to survive the SLORC takeover (the *Pyithu Hluttaw*, People's Assembly, and other institutions established by the 1974 socialist constitution having been rendered inoperative). In late September, the junta decreed a Political Party Registration Law, which opened the way for the establishment of literally hundreds of new political groups, of which only a handful, including the NLD, NUP and parties representing ethnic minorities such as the Arakanese and Shans, could be taken seriously.

The motive for Ne Win's initial suggestion was a mixture of desperation – his regime had its back to the wall in the face of massive popular demonstrations – and a desire on his part to distance himself from the failures of his own brand of home-grown socialism by promoting political as well as economic reform.[35] For the SLORC, the motive was economic. As mentioned above, it was strapped for cash and feared a split in the ranks of the *Tatmadaw*. By appearing to adhere to democratic norms, the junta could please foreign aid donors, especially Japan but also West Germany, Britain and the United States. Their best scenario was the election of compliant representatives, from the 'pro-government' NUP or a confusing array of small parties, who would rubber stamp *de facto* military control of a new 'democratic' political system.

In retrospect, this scenario was not improbable. Burma had held national elections for the *Pyithu Hluttaw* under the socialist system after the 1974 constitution was promulgated. Like elections in the Soviet Union and its Eastern European satellites, these were exercises in 'political education', ritualistic affirmations of the one-party regime's legitimacy, rather than free expressions of popular choice. The SLORC generals seemed to remain in the socialist mindset, despite market-oriented reforms. Through the medium of the Elections Commission, they established an elaborate procedural framework for balloting and under the Registration

Law, so many (about 233) parties were established, receiving government support in the form of gasoline rations and telephone lines, that the majority had to be 'de-registered' by the Commission, allowing only 93 parties to actually contest the election. Although the multi-party structure was different from the Soviet or BSPP model, the entire system was under the state's tight control. The SLORC had placed Aung San Suu Kyi under house arrest on 20 July 1989, removing its most popular and dangerous opponent. It was confident that the people, cowed by the use of armed force in 1988, would do what was expected of them. So confident, in fact, that the actual balloting was free and fair – as attested by foreign observers who monitored the proceedings and the results themselves.

The election ploy proved to be a major miscalculation, born of over-confidence and intelligence failures. What was most unsettling to Saw Maung and his fellow generals was that constituencies containing large numbers of *Tatmadaw* personnel, such as Rangoon's Mingaladon Township and the Cocos Islands, returned a large number of NLD parliamentarians.

The run-up to the election was fraught with ambiguity. It was never entirely clear what its exact *purpose* was: to choose a national assembly, and a government (as the NLD and most foreign governments assumed); or to elect a body that would draft a new constitution? On 22 September 1988, the SLORC's Secretary-1, Khin Nyunt (who was also head of the notorious Directorate of Defence Services Intelligence, or Military Intelligence), unequivocally stated: 'Once the elections are successfully completed, the Defence Forces will systematically hand over state power to the party that wins.'[36] According to the Pyithu Hluttaw Election Law decreed on 31 May 1989, 'The Hluttaw shall be formed with the Hluttaw representatives who have been elected in accordance with this law from the Hluttaw constituencies.'[37] But on 9 June 1989 the junta seemed to be moving, crabwise, away from its commitment to transfer power when an official spokesman stated that:

General Saw Maung ... had on numerous occasions touched on the matter of the transfer of power. He had stated that power would be transferred as soon as possible to a government that would emerge in accordance with law after the elections.

We do not know as yet to whom and how the power would be transferred, and we do not know who would win and in which manner we would transfer power. We cannot transfer power as soon as the elections are held. The government would be formed according to a constitution. If the state power is hurriedly transferred, it would lead to a shaky and weak government.[38]

The spokesman added to the confusion by saying that Burma had *two* constitutions, the post-war 1947 basic law and the 1974 constitution, and the elected representatives could choose which of the two to re-establish (since, under martial law, both constitutions were inoperative), *or* draft a new one. This would be, he asserted, their responsibility, not the junta's.[39] After the election was held, the victorious NLD representatives drafted and approved an interim basic law based on the 1947 constitution. But the SLORC reasserted its control of the situation by issuing Announcement No. 1/90, a decree that stated unequivocally that the military regime exercised full legislative, administrative (executive) and judicial powers, putting an end to talk about a transfer of power, at least in the near future.[40] It coupled this with a crackdown on the opposition, which resulted in most National League for Democracy leaders being put in jail.

When it became clear that the SLORC was not prepared to make way for a government of elected representatives, the Japanese Ministry of Foreign Affairs issued carefully worded statements expressing its concern that the popular will be respected.[41] On 30 August 1990, Watanabe Michio, the first member of the Diet to visit Burma after September 1988, met with General Saw Maung and urged the power transfer and release of Aung San Suu Kyi from house arrest.[42] Japanese officials took the occasion of the announcement of the award of the Nobel Peace Prize to Aung San Suu Kyi in October 1991 to press for her release and democratization.[43] In December 1991, Prime Minister Miyazawa Kiichi brought up the issue of Burma in a meeting with Malaysia's prime minister, Mahathir Mohammad, and the following month Watanabe, newly appointed foreign minister, broached the issue with China's deputy premier Wu Xueqian in Beijing.[44] But as the SLORC's crackdown on the opposition continued, Japan's quiet diplomacy seemed to have little positive effect.

Among the new military élite, attitudes toward Japan seemed cooler than those of the Ne Win generation. This was reflected in the junta's reaction to the visit by Sophia University Professor Ogata Sadako under United Nations auspices to investigate human rights conditions in November 1990. SLORC began a short but intense anti-Japanese campaign in the pages of its propaganda sheet, the *Working People's Daily*, including an article by 'Bo Thanmani' published during Professor Ogata's visit that described war atrocities by both the British and the Japanese and seemed to urge new war reparations 'because compensation paid by Japan to Burma after the war was the smallest [of Asian countries].'[45] An 'open letter' to Japan Socialist Party chairwoman Doi Takako by 'Maung Myanmar' (Brother Burman), published in December, claimed that no Burmese received compensation for suffering inflicted by Japan during the building of the Thai-Burma Railway, and Saw Maung took the occasion of Armed Forces Day on 27 March 1991 to remind officers and men of the misdeeds of the 'fascist Japanese'.[46]

Just before Ogata's November visit, the *Working People's Daily* published a crude cartoon (see Figure 4.1, next page) showing a determined *Tatmadaw*-man, armed with an automatic rifle, declaring 'I am two years old de facto government!' and towering over an clutch of diminutive foreigners: a stereotypical tubby Indian, forlorn caricatures of U.S. Senators Moynihan, Kennedy and Rohrabacher and Congressman Solarz demanding sanctions while noxious clouds labelled BBC, VOA (Voice of America) and AIR (All India Radio) hover over their heads – and to the Tatmadawman's left a small figure of a Japanese soldier wearing a toothpick-like samurai sword, nervously looking all around him and uttering *'taihen yoroshii, yoroshii'* [very fine, fine].[47]

Figure 4.1. This crude cartoon from the Working People's Daily, published on 5 October 1990, reflects cooler Burmese attitudes toward Japan: note the small figure of the Japanese soldier to the Tatmadawman's left

The regime treated the visiting human rights observer coolly, blocking her access to people who could report on rights abuses. Originally planning to stay at the Inya Lake Hotel, she was placed in a government guesthouse surrounded by armed guards, making it impossible for ordinary people to visit her. Low-level officials guided her to largely inconsequential sites in Rangoon's satellite towns that did not include the notorious Insein Jail, filled with political prisoners, or, as she had requested, a meeting with Aung San Suu Kyi. With the exception of Major General Khin Nyunt, members of the SLORC did not meet with her.[48] Some Japanese officials saw her shoddy treatment and the media references to wartime atrocities as deliberately insulting.[49] The regime initially refused entry to her successor as UN human rights investigator, International Christian University Professor Yokota Yōzō, and when he was finally allowed into the country, he, too, was denied an interview with Aung San Suu Kyi.[50]

AUNG SAN SUU KYI AND JAPAN

It is no exaggeration to say that in the eyes of the international community after 1988, Aung San Suu Kyi *was* Burma. Most articles about the country in newspapers and magazines – and by the mid-1990s the electronic media – focused on her contest of wills with the military regime, especially after she received the Nobel Peace Prize in 1991. Charismatic, attractive, and possessing undoubted courage, she put a human face on an exotic and largely unknown country. There were problems with the Suu Kyi-centred perspective: global concern about her treatment at the hands of the junta, including three terms of house arrest, has tended to overshadow other, larger-scale abuses, such as the regime's continued oppression of ethnic minorities such as the Karens and Shans whose plight only occasionally makes it into the mainstream media. But this was certainly not her intention, and without her, Burma after 1988 would probably have slipped back into obscurity, like Sudan or the Congo.

She quickly became the most popular figure in the opposition, especially after giving her speech at the Shwe Dagon Pagoda on 26 August. As mentioned in Chapter Two, the speech described the popular movement against the Ne Win regime as 'the second struggle for national independence'.[51] Her rapid rise to prominence reflected her own talents and her resemblance to her universally revered father, but it also highlighted Burma's political vacuum. After 1962, there were no credible political leaders to challenge the old dictator. None of the surviving 'Thirty Comrades' took a decisive political role. The new generation of student activists like Min Ko Naing were quickly rounded up and put in jail, or fled the country. Her strongest rival, retired Brigadier Aung Gyi, criticised her for lack of experience, but the public viewed him as untrustworthy and too subservient to his old commander Ne Win.[52]

Daw Suu Kyi was, in the words of one Burmese observer, an 'accidental tourist' who, returning after many years abroad to look after her ailing mother, became a political leader almost overnight. Because of SLORC repression after the election, including the jailing of hundreds of party members, her NLD was unable to develop new leadership or an organisational infrastructure that would have made it more effective. Most of the NLD's other leaders, such as U Tin U and U Kyi Maung, were conservative retired *Tatmadaw* officers with limited popular appeal. The party's existence depended almost entirely on her popularity and international prestige – even, if not especially – when she was under house arrest.

This unnatural situation – an environment in which there was a dearth of political alternatives and millions of ordinary Burmese looked to the 'Goddess on University Avenue' for inspiration[53] – gave the country's politics an intensely personal hue. Outside of Burma, to support democracy meant to support and revere 'the Lady'. Her international stature brought into question the morality of business-as-usual with the military regime. Conversely, business interests who argued for constructive engagement with the SLORC/ SPDC found her an obstacle, and sought to 'demythologize' and even defame her, a movement that became increasingly apparent by the late 1990s.

Japanese leaders found they couldn't ignore her. Her father's close historical connection with Japan gave him a central place in the popular image of Burma as 'the friendliest country in Asia toward Japan'. Daw Suu Kyi had undertaken research on his life at the Centre for Southeast Asian Studies of Kyoto University, including interviews with former members of the Japanese military. During her nine months there in 1985–1986, she gained a reputation for quiet diligence, and the Centre's director, Professor Yano Toru, expressed surprise upon seeing her on the television news during Democracy Summer, 'quite a different, militant Suu Kyi' who had been given the opportunity to put her political ideals, inspired by Mahatma Gandhi and Dr. Martin Luther King, into action. In 'Reflections on Suu Kyi's Nobel Peace Prize', he enjoined his colleagues to pray 'for Suu Kyi's safety, for Burma's political maturity, and for the support of people of conscience across the world for Suu Kyi's solitary struggle' under house arrest.[54]

Members of both houses of the Diet submitted petitions requesting Daw Suu Kyi's release from house arrest. In April 1994, *The Japan Times* reported that more than half the Diet membership, 403 out of 763 representatives, signed a petition to the United Nations Secretary General in coordination with similar petitions from other countries.[55] Members of the Diet, including Eda Satsuki and Hatoyama Yukio, organised a 'Parliamentary Coalition to Seek the Release of Aung San Suu Kyi'. Its activities included coordination with parliamentarians in other countries and sponsoring study sessions on the struggle for democracy in Burma.[56]

Especially after she became a Nobel laureate, books by or about Daw Suu Kyi were published in Japan, including a translation of her essays, *Freedom from Fear*, and a collection of her speeches.[57] She even made it into the world of *manga*, Japanese book length comics (Figure 4.2). In 1994, a *manga* publisher came out with the story of her life in the 'Super Nobel Prize Story' series. Titled *Aung San Suu Kyi, Tatakau kujaku* [Aung San Suu Kyi, the fighting

Figure 4.2. A young Aung San Suu Kyi goes to Oxford. From *Aung San Suu Kyi, the fighting peacock*, a *manga* published in 1994.

peacock], it begins with the assassination of her father when she was two years old and ends with her receiving the Peace Prize in 1991. There is also a detailed depiction of the events of Democracy Summer, including her speech at the Shwe Dagon Pagoda, and her 1989 house arrest. But Daw Suu Kyi and her British husband Michael Aris are portrayed in the typical *manga* style as *bishōnen* (beautiful young people), with innocently cute faces and big (in her case, very un-Asian) round eyes, meant to make them more appealing to Japanese readers.[58]

In the early 1990s, the broadcast media, including the state-owned television network NHK (Nihon Hōsō Kyōkai), gave her extensive coverage. In a 1991 historical programme on wartime Japanese assistance to the Burmese independence movement, for example, she was mentioned as the daughter of Aung San, indicating that she is the inheritor of his patriotic legacy.[59] Commercial television stations such as the Tokyo Broadcasting System (TBS) also produced news features and programmes on the pro-democracy leader: for example, TBS's Sunday evening news analysis programme, *Jōhō Tokushū* [News special edition].[60] In the early 1990s, Japanese newspapers, especially the more liberal dailies such as the *Asahi Shimbun* and the *Mainichi Shimbun*, paid more attention to her than did their counterparts in the West such as *The New York Times*. After Daw Suu Kyi's release from house arrest in July 1995, the *Mainichi Shimbun* published her weekly 'Letter from Burma' in Japanese translation, which also appeared in the English language *Mainichi Daily News*. In 1996, the series won an award from the Japan Publishers' and Editors' Association.[61]

If Daw Suu Kyi's international stature and her popularity within Japan precluded business-as-usual, it also made 'quiet dialogue' between the SLORC and the Japanese government superficially simple. For the junta, she became a bargaining chip in their efforts to secure more Japanese ODA. For Tokyo, progress toward democratization was defined over-simply in terms of their treatment of her. The SLORC's unexpected decision to release her from house arrest in July 1995 reflected their belief that substantial rewards would result from what was, against the background of their numerous other human rights abuses, a token gesture. This, again, was not her intention. 'What', a correspondent from the *Far Eastern Economic Review* asked her in August 1995, 'do you think about Japan's decision to resume aid?' (referring to a statement by the Japanese government after her release that it was considering such a resumption):

> [Suu Kyi]: I think they should wait and see a bit and not rush into it. Aid should get to people who need it most and it should be given in the right way at the right time. If it is a reward for my release, I'm just one political prisoner released, and there are others as well. The change in condition of just one person is not enough.[62]

NOTES

[1] Lintner (1989: 98, 242, 243).

[2] Lintner (1989: 15, 16, 101). Journalist Bertil Lintner's *Outrage: Burma's Struggle for Democracy* remains, after 17 years, the authoritative account of the events of 1988.

[3] Comment of informant to author, Rangoon, March 2004.

[4] Selth (1989).

[5] Earlier demonetization orders in 1964 and 1985 had provided at least partial compensation, if old notes were turned in to state banks.

[6] Comment of informant to author, Rangoon, March 2004; and Kyaw Yin Hlaing (2003: 53–56).

[7] Lintner (1989: 119).

[8] As martial law was declared in Rangoon on 3 August, the military rather than the Riot Police were responsible for enforcing order.

[9] By contrast, Mandalay was administered during Democracy Summer by a single provisional government headed by Buddhist monks. Comment of informant to author, Rangoon, March 2004.

[10] In the Basic Principles of the State, the constitution outline approved by the national Convention in 1996, the military is guaranteed a quarter of the seats in the national legislature and immunity from civilian oversight.

[11] Address by Ms. Takahashi Taeko, Director of the First Southeast Asia Division, MoFA, in Mekong Watch (2001: 15).

[12] Ibid.

[13] *Daily Report: East Asia* (1988); *Daily Report: East Asia* (1988a).

[14] Lintner (1989: 250).

[15] Inada (1990: 57, 58).

[16] *Biruma Jōhō (Myanmā Nyūsu)* (1988: 15).

[17] Ibid.

[18] Lintner (1989: 195).

[19] Comment of retired Japanese official to author, Tokyo, 21 August 1991. Mrs. Ohtaka, also known as Yamaguchi Yoshiko, was a colourful character. During the war, she was a popular film star known by the Chinese name Li Ko-ran (Li Xianglan) and after 1945 she did a stint in Hollywood as Shirley Yamaguchi. Aside from chairing the Nihon–

Biruma Kyōkai, she was a member of the Upper House of the Japanese Diet. It is unclear whether she shared her husband's opinions about Ne Win and the SLORC.

20 Lintner (1989: 226; 1989a: 13). The Japanese, American, British, West German, Italian and French ambassadors 'by coincidence' flew out of Rangoon to avoid the ceremony.

21 *Biruma Joohoo (Myanmaa Nyusu)* (1989: 6, 7), quoting the state-run *Working People's Daily*, 7 March 1989.

22 Lintner (1989: 254, 255); comment of retired Japanese official to author, Tokyo, 21 August 1991.

23 Iida Tsuneo, Nagoya University. *Gaik Foramu* (1988).

24 Haruna Kazuo, Marubeni Corporation. Ibid.

25 Comment of U.S. State Department official to author, Okinawa, 17 September 1992.

26 *Working People's Daily* (1989). According to a Japanese Burma specialist interviewed by this writer in February 1990, Ohtaka was opposed to the decision to normalize relations, but as ambassador could not state this publicly. His term as ambassador ended in December 1989.

27 Richburg (1989).

28 *Daily Report: East Asia* (1989d).

29 *Daily Report: East Asia* (1989c).

30 *Daily Report: East Asia:* (1989b).

31 Holloway (1989: 20, 21).

32 Saitō (1992: 22, 23). A civilian, Dr. Pe Thein, minister of health and education, led the Burmese delegation to the funeral.

33 Comment of Japanese Ministry of Foreign Affairs official to author, Tokyo, 6 February 1991.

34 It was widely and perhaps erroneously perceived among activists that international sanctions caused the collapse of the *apartheid* regime in the late 1980s.

35 In his later years (Ne Win died in late 2002), the old dictator seemed to have been obsessed by his place in Burmese history.

36 *Daily Report: East Asia* (1988b).

37 Weller (1993: 149).

[38] Ibid., pp. 147, 148.

[39] Ibid.

[40] Ibid., 194–196.

[41] Japan. Ministry of Foreign Affairs (1990).

[42] *Daily Report: East Asia* (1990: 45). Watanabe, who served as minister of international trade and industry in a Liberal Democratic Party cabinet, was an influential advocate of closer trade ties between Japan and Southeast Asia and visited Burma as part of his trip to the region.

[43] *Nihon Keizai Shimbun* (1991); *Mainichi Shimbun* (1991).

[44] *Mainichi Shimbun* (1991a); *Yomiuri Shimbun* (1992).

[45] Thanmani, Bo (1990).

[46] 'Maung Myanmar' (1990); *Working People's Daily* (1991).

[47] *Working People's Daily* (1990).

[48] *Daily Report: East Asia* (1990a: 28); *Daily Report: East Asia* (1990b: 41).

[49] Comment by official, Japan Ministry of Foreign Affairs, to author, Tokyo, 6 June 1991.

[50] *Far Eastern Economic Review* (1991: 8).

[51] Aung San Suu Kyi (1995: 193).

[52] After quitting the NLD in December 1988, he established his own party, the Union Nationals Democracy Party, but it won only one seat in the May 1990 election. Aged former prime minister U Nu's attempt to establish a 'parallel government' with himself as leader in September 1988 was greeted with almost universal scepticism, and his party, the League for Democracy and Peace, failed to win a single seat.

[53] *Thekkado yeittha lan ga Nat Thami* in Burmese, referring to the street on which her residence was located. See Nemoto (1996: 8–10) for an interesting discussion of Daw Suu Kyi and traditional Burmese mystical beliefs.

[54] Yano (1991: 3).

[55] *The Japan Times* (1994).

[56] Amnesty International-Japan Branch (1995: 85, 86).

[57] Aung San Suu Kyi (1991a); Aung San Suu Kyi (1996).

[58] Akazu (1994).

[59] NHK (1991).

[60] TBS (1994).

[61] *Mainichi Daily News* (1996b).

[62] Fairclough (1995: 26).

Chapter Five

THE AMBIGUITIES OF 'QUIET DIALOGUE'

The political crisis in Burma stimulated the emergence of constituencies within the Japanese political system who competed for influence over the government's Burma policy. Traditional business interests who had benefited from ODA as a 'boomerang economy' in the past, as represented by the membership of the Nihon–Biruma Kyōkai (renamed the Nihon–Myanmar Kyōkai to reflect the SLORC's 1989 change in the country's official name), advocated closer economic engagement with the post-socialist regime for reasons outlined in the Association's 1989 petition. Their agenda was also reflected in the May 1998 establishment of a parliamentarians' group, the 'League to Encourage Support for the Myanmar Government', headed by a prominent member of the Liberal Democratic Party, Mutō Kabun. Mutō gave a strategic rationale for restoration of the pre-1988 status quo: 'Because it is coming under China's influence, Myanmar may have conflict with India, causing regional instability. In order to avoid this, it is necessary for Japan to support the present government, including the reopening of yen loans.'[1]

Business interests remained strong, but not unchallenged. A much smaller 'democracy and human rights' constituency – such as the Japan branch of Amnesty International, the Association of Burmese in Japan and the People's Forum on Burma – wanted Tokyo to take greater initiative in promoting political change. Lacking influence within ruling circles, such groups were easy for the Japanese government to ignore; but it could not ignore the opinions of the United States government, which held similar views and had possibly pressured Japan to take a harder line during 1988. By the mid-1990s, the administration of President Bill Clinton was deeply committed to backing Aung San Suu Kyi. Clinton's secretary of state, Madeleine Albright, had visited the pro-democracy leader in Rangoon after her release from house arrest in 1995 and took a strong personal interest in her welfare. Japan's Ministry of Foreign Affairs found itself in a delicate situation, having to accommodate domestic and international constituencies with conflicting agendas at a time when its optimal scenario, economic *and* political reform by the SLORC, was not working out.

JAPANESE BUSINESS IN POST-SOCIALIST BURMA

One of the most important interventions in Burma by Japanese parties after 1988 came not from the government, but from a small company, Mimatsu Construction Group (MCG), which purchased land belonging to the Burmese embassy in Tokyo's Shinagawa Ward in 1989–1990. Before the collapse of the 'bubble economy', Tokyo land prices were sky-high, and the sale netted the junta ¥60.0 billion (US$435 million), a much-appreciated infusion of cash at a time when the new regime was struggling for its economic survival.[2] In 1990, MCG secured a joint venture contract to build a US$45 million hotel in Rangoon.[3] Details of the embassy land transaction are obscure: apart from MCG, one of the important participants in the transaction was the head of Sanwa Trading, a company that established an early presence in Rangoon in areas such as the export of seafood.[4]

During the early 1990s, Japanese companies operating in Burma could be generally placed in one of two categories: small firms like MCG and Sanwa, working outside the Japanese business mainstream, which dared to enter a highly risky business environment; and the major general trading companies (*sōgō shōsha*) which are at the heart of the business establishment, have a long historical connection with the country and adopted a watch-and-wait attitude, keeping their offices in Rangoon open. Well-known Japanese manufacturing firms were generally wary of entering the Burmese market on their own because of the risks involved and potential damage to their international image by engaging with the SLORC.

One of the oddest cases was Daichi, an obscure manufacturer of signboards headed by Bernard Choi, a person of Korean ethnicity who among other things had been a business partner of Neil Bush, errant son of President George H. W. Bush.[5] In June 1990, Choi signed a joint venture agreement with the SLORC to establish the Myanmar-Concord Development Organisation (MCDO). According to the *Bangkok Post*, MCDO planned to construct 'an entire new city' in the Rangoon area including a new airport, 'almost 4,000 man-made lakes', resorts, a highway system, high technology telecommunications and a total investment of over US$15 billion over 15 years. It was envisioned that the new city would have a population as high as four million by 2001.[6] MCDO established an office in the plush Akasaka district of central Tokyo, but by 1992 Choi's grandiose plans had evaporated and its office was closed.[7]

Small Japanese firms were active in one of the liveliest and most visible export sectors, the sale of second-hand Japanese buses for use as public transportation in Rangoon and other cities. Often, the recycled vehicles kept their original Japanese markings, including destination signs in *kanji* (Chinese characters), which Burmese riders may have found pleasingly exotic. But they presented a serious safety problem. As was (and is) the case in Japan, vehicles in Burma originally drove on the left hand side of the road, but for obscure astrological reasons Ne Win decreed in the 1970s that vehicles suddenly switch to driving on the right hand side. This meant that unless a new door was cut on the right hand side of the imported buses, passengers had to alight on the left, in the middle of the street rather than on the pavement. While South Korean buses, from a country that drives on the right, were plausible alternatives, Japanese buses remained popular in the early twenty-first century.[8] There was also great demand for used cars, especially Toyota sedans that could be recycled as taxis, and second-hand Japanese-made television sets and stereos, which were a lot cheaper than new, but still reliable.

The *sōgō shōsha* anticipated an improvement in the business as well as political environment that would lead to Tokyo's approval of new ODA. The Marubeni trading firm had a major share in procurement contracts for the stalled Mingaladon Airport modernization project, the biggest single Japanese aid project, and hoped it would be re-started. According to one observer, the general trading companies, enjoying access to local power holders and other sources of information, also acted as 'an unofficial proxy for the Japanese government, which for political reasons cannot cooperate too closely with the ruling junta'.[9]

At no time after 1988 was the Burmese economic situation more promising than in 1994–1997: foreign private investment was booming and Burma's GDP was growing at rates comparable to its ASEAN neighbours. Burma's ambition to become a member of the Association of South East Asian Nations (accomplished in July 1997) promised the rewards of regional economic integration. It was at this time that major Japanese companies, especially the *sōgō shōsha*, stepped up the momentum for economic engagement. In June 1994, Keidanren (the Federation of Economic Organisations), the most important business association in Japan, sent a special delegation to Rangoon headed by Marubeni chairman Haruna Kazuo. Haruna and other mission members, numbering fifty, met with top SLORC and government leaders including junta chairman Senior General Than Shwe, Secretary-1 Khin Nyunt, and economic planning minister David O. Abel. Fêted and feasted, the Keidanren group saw a video showing anti-government *jacquerie* decapitating a suspected police informer in the streets of Rangoon in 1988. Haruna expressed shock that people could do such atrocious things.[10] The choice of a Marubeni executive as the mission's head was no accident. His successor as Marubeni chairman, Toriumi Iwao, served as chairman of Keidanren's Japan–Myanmar Economic Committee, established in May 1996.[11]

Keidanren led the way for other high-profile Japanese companies to establish a presence in the country. In late 1994, Daiwa Securities, one of Japan's 'big four' security trading houses, signed a memorandum of understanding with the SLORC to assist in setting up a Rangoon stock exchange.[12] In August 1995, the Tokyo-Mitsubishi Bank reopened its Rangoon office (it had been closed since the mid-1980s). A few months later, it was followed by Fuji, Tokai, Sumitomo and Sanwa Banks.[13] In February 1996, Mitsui Bussan (Mitsui Trading Company) made an agreement with the SLORC's ministry of construction to build a 9,600 square meter industrial park in the northern outskirts of Rangoon;[14] and in July of that year, All Nippon Airways, Japan's second largest airline, began direct flights between Kansai Airport and Rangoon.

In April 1996, Mitsui Bussan joined with the American and French oil companies Unocal and Total to sign a memorandum of understanding with the SLORC for the so-called 'three-in-one project', valued at US$800 million: to construct a pipeline from the off-shore Yadana Natural Gas Field to Rangoon; connection of the pipeline to a new electric power plant; and construction of a urea fertilizer production facility which would also utilize natural gas from Yadana.[15] Mitsui's connection with Yadana was controversial. Critics claimed that the participating companies were complicit in *Tatmadaw* human rights violations such as forced labour and forced relocation in ethnic minority areas traversed by the original Yadana pipeline, which crossed through Tenasserim Division before reaching Thailand, where the gas would be used for power generation. In addition, Nippon Oil of Japan became a partner, along with Premier Oil of Britain, the Petroleum Authority of Thailand, Petronas of Malaysia and the Myanmar Oil and Gas Enterprise (MOGE), in the development of the Yetagun well, located south of the Yadana well in the Andaman Sea. The Yetagun project also included transport of the gas through the overland Burma–Thailand pipeline and, like the Yadana project, has been implicated in human rights abuses.[16]

'SUU KYI BASHING'

As will be discussed below, the Japanese government continued to exercise self-restraint on new ODA projects – that is, no *new* yen loans – for political, diplomatic and economic reasons. As it became clear to business interests that the golden years of the Burmese 'boomerang economy' were over, prominent figures began engaging in what Nagai Hiroshi called 'Suu Kyi bashing' (*Suu Kyi bashingu* in Japanese).[17] One example is author Fukada Yusuke, writing in 1995 in the well-known monthly *Bungei Shunjū*, who claimed that the SLORC was sending passionate 'love calls' to Japan asking for development aid, but that these calls had been ignored because of the 'Suu Kyi problem (*Suu Kyi to iu mondai*)', namely, that Daw Suu Kyi refused to compromise with the military regime. Fukada claimed that this was because she was married to an Englishman. If she had been married to a Japanese, she would have acted in a very different way. Another writer he cites is Keio University professor Kusano Atsushi, whose article 'Amazement over the view of Suu Kyi as a heroine' was published in 1996 in *Shokun* magazine; it claimed that the international media largely invented her heroic image, and that the military regime had not been given credit for its accomplishments. Although Nagai acknowledges that there has been conscientious reporting in the Japanese media about Burma, the main focus has been on the views of power holders and business élites.[18]

The most renowned Japanese business figure attempting to 'demythologise' Daw Suu Kyi was Ohmae Kenichi, management guru and advocate of the magic of the global marketplace who claimed, in the 1997 year-end issue of *Asiaweek* magazine, that:

The West knows about Myanmar through one person, Aung San Suu Kyi. The obsession with Suu Kyi is a natural one if you understand the U.S. Superficial democracy is golden in the United States; American love elections. Just as Myanmar is Buddhist, and Malaysia is Islamic, America has a religion called Democracy. There is merit in promoting democratic reforms. But America is a simplistic country. Americans insist that what works for them should work for others at any time and in any stage of economic development.[19]

Ohmae explored further the linkage between Daw Suu Kyi and the allegedly simple-minded American notions about democracy in two November 1997 articles published in *Sapio*, a right-wing Japanese magazine. In 'Mrs. Suu Kyi is becoming a burden for developing Myanmar', he claimed that the United States 'has established her as the Jeanne d'Arc of Myanmar and is using her to spread their propaganda and pressure the regime. However, why the US feels the need to do this and to achieve what end is beyond my comprehension.'[20] He believed that in a couple of years, Burma's extraordinary economic progress under military rule would make her 'a person of the past'.

One visit to the country made Ohmae a zealous convert, though exactly how much he saw of it is unclear. He praised Burma's 'fervently Buddhist ethics', its safe streets ('Besides Japan and Singapore, Myanmar is one of the safest places to walk alone at night' and 'murder cases have been unheard of in recent years'), and spectacular improvements in local infrastructure. For example, it used to take 'hours' to drive from Rangoon to the ancient capital city of Pagan, but you can make the trip over a newly paved highway in 'two hours' (as a quick glance at a map of the country shows, this assumes an average speed of around 150 miles an hour!). 'Villages', he claimed, 'are extremely clean. There are no slums. This is due to the lack of difference in wealth'[21] – statements that suggest Ohmae was too busy listening to SLORC spokesmen in air-conditioned seminar rooms to venture into downtown Rangoon or its satellite towns, the places where thousands of desperately poor people had fought the *Tatmadaw* in 1988. If anything is true of the post-socialist economy, it is that in Burma, gaps between rich and poor have widened tremendously. Even Aung San Suu Kyi has admitted that compared with the present situation, education and health conditions during the Ne Win era were not all that bad.

In this article and a second one, 'Cheap and hardworking labourers: this country will be Asia's best', Ohmae indulged in a fascinating exercise in Orientalism, Japanese-style, which echoes the idylls of *Harp of Burma*. He contrasted Burmese Buddhist values with the 'money-worshipping capitalism' of China and Vietnam, in which everyone is obsessed with accumulating material goods and getting rich quickly. Burmese villages reminded him of his own childhood in the countryside of Kyushu, 'where children always walked around barefoot, the lights were not electric, and the bathrooms had no running water'.[22] Yet all of this was seamlessly reconciled with the author's own sharp eye for the bottom line: 'Myanmar's wages are about a half to a tenth of other Asian nations.' Burmese are well-educated (despite their poverty), fluent in English, and 'conscientious and sincere from beginning to end' (unlike the Chinese, who 'on the surface … appear sincere and serious, but in reality they do everything for money'). At the close of his 26 November *Sapio* article, Ohmae asked that young Japanese people go to Burma and see the situation for themselves: 'I would like for them to confirm that reality in Myanmar is completely different from the image portrayed by Japanese and American media as "military dictatorship – repression – poor Suu Kyi"'.[23]

Ohmae wanted his readers to believe that it was Daw Suu Kyi, and America, who kept all of Burma's good things (cheap, docile labourers; rich natural resources; and a military regime intent on economic liberalization) tantalisingly out of reach. Yet objective economic conditions played the major role in limiting Japanese private economic engagement as the decade of the 1990s came to a close. Although Japan remained an important source of Burmese imports (including used vehicles), it ranked an unimpressive ninth among sources of private foreign investment approvals (US$219 million). Japan was not only behind Singapore (number one at US$1.485 billion), Thailand (US$1.237 billion) and Malaysia (US$587 million), but also – ironically, given their support of a hard line against the junta – behind Britain (US$1.352 billion) and the United States (US$582 million).[24] A number of Japanese firms closed down or postponed their operations in Burma, including Mitsui's involvement in the Yadana 'three-in-one' project.[25] All Nippon Airways suspended its Kansai–Rangoon service in early 2000.

Largely because of *economic* factors, Japanese companies found the Burmese business environment excessively risky, though the underlying factor was *political* – not the 'Suu Kyi problem' but the junta's determination to monopolise power in virtually all areas of national life, including business.

In 1998, Keidanren's Japan–Myanmar Economic Committee conducted a survey of Japanese companies operating in the country and discovered agreement on three major problems: the poor quality of infrastructure; a 'dual exchange rate system'; and lack of information and transparency concerning the government's policies.[26] The exchange rate system was especially confusing: after 1988, the highly overvalued official rate for the *kyat*, around K6 to the US dollar, was retained, but was no longer uniformly enforced; dollars could also be exchanged for *kyat* on the street for a much more favourable rate (as much as over K1,100=US$1.00 in 2005, when the government wasn't cracking down on speculators). The government also established special *kyat*-dollar exchange rates between the official and free market rates for the payment of fees and customs duties. Economists saw this complex system as an irrational obstacle to trade and investment, but the SLORC retained it largely for political reasons: the military elite and well-connected business people could use their *kyats* to buy foreign currency at the generous official rate, while ordinary Burmese had to buy dollars on the free market at a rate that could be over a hundred times more unfavourable. By controlling who got which rate, the government wielded a powerful economic incentive. The credibility of the *kyat* was also undermined by the SLORC's use of the printing press to cover budget shortfalls, especially when *Tatmadaw* personnel and civil servants were given pay increases. This contributed to chronic inflation, which undercut living standards for ordinary people.

By the early twenty-first century, it had become clear that the State Peace and Development Council, as the junta was renamed in 1997, was not delivering on its promises of economic reform.[27] It had replaced state socialism with state capitalism. Major enterprises were controlled by military-owned entities such as the Union of

Myanmar Economic Holdings. Top generals issued economic decrees without the advice of competent technocratic advisers. For example, a sudden ban in April 2002 on exports and imports by foreign trading companies caused 20 to 30 firms, including two Japanese trading companies, to suspend their operations.[28] Apart from the junta's lingering socialist mindset, a major factor was China's economic support for the regime and its business cronies. Because Chinese economic engagement was both large-scale and had no strings attached (apart from profits for the investors), there was little sense of urgency on the junta's part to carry out market-oriented reforms or establish a consistently enforced legal framework for business operations. When a military officer serving as deputy minister of economic planning and development, Brigadier Zaw Tun, criticised the SPDC for its failures in economic reform in July 2000, he was summarily dismissed.[29]

It was not surprising that the most successful ventures were in the 'quick and dirty' exploitation of Burma's abundant natural resources in remote maritime and border areas: not only teak, fisheries and natural gas, but also opium, which through elaborate money-laundering channels, often involving Chinese intermediaries, provided infusions of cash for regime-related business interests even if the top generals were not directly involved. As long as these enterprises, especially natural gas exports to Thailand, brought the SPDC large revenues, there was even less incentive for them to carry out economic reform.[30]

THE JAPANESE AID PRESENCE IN BURMA AFTER 1988

Quantitatively, Tokyo remained Burma's largest donor of aid after normalisation in 1989, disbursing an average sum of US$63.7 million annually and a total of US$827.9 million in the 1989–2001 period (see Table 3.1, p. 62ff.). During this period, Japanese ODA was equivalent to 78.7 per cent of all bilateral aid disbursed by the OECD's Development Assistance Committee (DAC). Between 1970 and 1988, as mentioned in Chapter Three, Japanese loans and

---

Japan in the 'Golden Triangle'

One of the more unusual Japanese grant projects during the late 1990s was a programme, begun with the initiative of influential Liberal Democratic Party parliamentarian Katō Kōichi, to promote the eradication of opium poppy cultivation in Kokang, a Shan State district located close to the Chinese border. In place of poppies, Kokang farmers would cultivate *soba* (buckwheat), which is used in popular Japanese noodle dishes, as a substitute crop. It began in 1996 when LDP adviser Iwakura Tomomitsu and agricultural scientist Ujihara Akio met with SLORC Secretary-1 Khin Nyunt, who since 1989 had been in control of 'Border Area Development' programmes. The following year, *soba* was grown on an experimental basis on two acres, and by 2000, the area had expanded to 3,000 acres. Iwakura and Ujihara hoped that a market for Burmese *soba* could be opened in Japan, and in December 1999, the Japanese ambassador in Rangoon, Asakai Kazuo, invited top SPDC and government officials to a traditional buckwheat noodle dinner at his residence.

Rigorous opium suppression policies carried out by the Kokang local authorities caused great hardship among farmers, who had no other source of income, and it was unclear whether *soba* could provide them with an adequate substitute income. Moreover, given the strongly protected nature of Japanese agricultural markets, the appeal of buckwheat grown in a little-known Third World Country was questionable. Perhaps the most striking feature of the project was that Tokyo initiated it in an area that traditionally has been China's sphere of influence, and it showed close connections between influential Japanese, including the LDP's Katō, and the allegedly 'reformist' Khin Nyunt, who was purged in 2004. – *See*: *Asahi Shimbun* (2003); Japan International Cooperation Agency (2001).

---

grants were about two thirds (66.5 per cent) of all DAC bilateral disbursements, though aid totals during this period were much higher than after 1988 (an annual average of US$102.3 million from Japan in 1970–1988). After 1988, new loan projects were not approved (they had not been approved since 1986), with the arguable exception of ¥2.5 billion in the 1997 fiscal year, but some old ODA that was in the pipeline was allowed to flow. There were also grants, largely for humanitarian and debt relief purposes.

Several large projects were finished after 1988. One was the Ngawun Bridge, located near Rangoon, which was initially funded by a ¥1.5 billion grant in 1986. Its completion in 1992 was described by *The Japan Times* as a 'major success in technology transfer', since Burmese rather than Japanese engineers played the major role in its construction. A comment by one of the engineers, however, suggested another state of affairs: 'Because there are many rivers in our country, we have to construct many more bridges. *If we can get construction material from Japan* [italics added], we are confident that we can build longer bridges.'[31] In June 1992, work was resumed on another large project, the Nawin Dam, located near the city of Prome (Pyay) in central Burma and funded by a ¥8 billion loan. The dam was completed in 1995.[32] But the largest aid project, modernization and expansion of Rangoon's Mingaladon Airport, remained uncompleted. While Japanese-made heavy equipment quietly rusted on the construction site, major technical and political obstacles frustrated the resumption of the ¥27 billion project.[33]

Debt relief grants constituted a major portion of post-1988 Japanese ODA: a total of ¥67.97 billion or approximately US$573 million between 1990 and 2002 (at an average 1990–2000 exchange rate of ¥118.7=US$1). Strictly speaking, this was not new aid, or even payments to the recipient country, since the Japanese government gave these grants only after an equivalent amount of debt had been serviced in hard currency by the SLORC/SPDC. This system began in the late 1970s when, following United Nations initiatives, Tokyo began giving the grants to eleven of the poorest countries so they could pay for imports of oil. Observers were critical of the debt relief grants because Japanese government regulations required that the grant funds had to be used to purchase imports; since they were denominated in yen, it was natural that they would benefit Japanese suppliers.[34] Thus, the importance of debt relief grants in Tokyo's post-1988 aid presence could be interpreted not only as a series of confidence-building measures that affirmed Tokyo's willingness to lessen Burma's debt burden and Rangoon's determination to deal with its financial obligations (thus gratifying the Ministry of Finance), but also as a means of sustaining the Japanese 'boomerang economy' in Burma at a time when big yen loan projects were still infeasible. However, in December 2002 foreign minister Kawaguchi Yoriko announced that the debt cancellation system would be reformed: rather than converting loan payments into grants, the Japan Bank for International Cooperation would simply write off the debt when it falls due.[35]

A number of Japanese technical specialists were sent to Burma, and Burmese nationals accepted for training or study programs in Japan. During 1989–2003, budget approvals for the former were in the range of 21 to 516 in different years, while the latter ranged between ten and 670 (and 398 *ryūgakusei* or exchange students), respectively (see Table 5.1, p. 128ff.).

JAPANESE ODA AND DEMOCRATIZATION

As discussed in the previous chapter, the Japanese government's policy toward Burma after it recognised the SLORC in February 1989 was based on the optimistic assumption that the regime was serious about political and economic reform and that a transition to some form of civilian government and market-oriented economics was imminent. *De facto* annulment of the May 1990 election brought this optimism into question; but Tokyo continued, through its policy of 'quiet dialogue', to deal with the military regime using a combination of mild expressions of moral support for Aung San Suu Kyi and allocation of not insignificant amounts of aid, as discussed above, to indicate that much larger allocations were in the works if the situation inside Burma improved. Such a policy was fraught with ambiguity. The Japanese government expressed its principles in only the most vague terms, their application was frustratingly inconsistent, and the decision-making process behind them was far from transparent. Yet as will be explained below, neither the ambiguities of 'quiet dialogue' nor the hard line approach taken by the United States, which had its own ambiguities and loopholes, has had a major impact on the behaviour of the military regime. It happily accepts Japanese carrots, and has become increasingly skilful at dodging western sticks with the help of China and ASEAN.

Table 5.1: The Japanese Aid Presence in Burma, 1989–2003 (unit: 100 million yen)

Year	Loans	Grants	Technical cooperation	TOTAL[1]
1989	0	0	1.29 (11 Burmese trainees in Japan; 30 Japanese specialists in Burma)	1.29 [$935,000]
1990	0	35.0 (1 debt relief grant)	3.74 (22 Burmese trainees in Japan; 57 Japanese specialists in Burma)	38.74 [$26.7 million]
1991	0	50.0 (2 debt relief grants)	3.87 (16 Burmese trainees in Japan; 29 Japanese specialists in Burma)	53.87 [$40.0 million]
1992	0	40.0 (2 debt relief grants)	4.08 (10 Burmese trainees in Japan; 21 Japanese specialists in Burma)	44.08 [$34.8 million]
1993	0	62.0 (3 debt relief grants); 0.18 (grass roots projects)[2]	3.24 (11 Burmese trainees in Japan; 21 Japanese specialists in Burma)	65.42 [$58.9 million]
1994	0	120.0 (3 debt relief grants); 10.0 (aid for increased food production); 0.42 (grass roots projects)	3.98 (45 Burmese trainees in Japan; 53 Japanese specialists in Burma)	134.4 [$131.5 million]
1995	0	140.0 (3 debt relief grants); 16.25 (renovation of Institute of Nursing, Rangoon); 2.0 (aid for increased food production); 0.74 (grass roots projects)[2]	5.99 (64 Burmese trainees in Japan; 57 Japanese specialists in Burma)	165.0 [$175.6 million]

1996	0	80.0 (2 debt relief grants); 0.97 (grass roots projects)	4.93 (69 Burmese trainees in Japan; 33 Japanese specialists in Burma)	85.9 [$79.0 million]
1997	25.0[3] (Rangoon airport modernization)	40.0 (2 debt relief grants); 1.17 (grass roots projects); 0.05 (emergency assistance)	6.33 (81 Burmese trainees in Japan; 33 Japanese specialists in Burma)	72.55 [$59.9 million]
1998	0	40.0 (2 debt relief grants); 8.0 (aid for increased food production); 3.3 (mother-child healthcare improvement); 1.62 (grass roots projects)	7.68 (137 Burmese trainees in Japan; 69 Japanese specialists in Burma)	60.6 [$46.3 million]
1999	0	15.86 (1 debt relief grant); 5.97 (mother-child healthcare improvement); 2.88 (grass roots projects)	10.86 (123 Burmese trainees in Japan; 125 Japanese specialists in Burma)	35.6 [$31.3 million]
2000	0	17.77 (1 debt relief grant); 6.73 (mother-child healthcare improvement); 6.24 (Shan State water sanitation project); 4.11 (grass roots projects); 2.25 (equipment for Rangoon General Hospital); 0.4 (equipment for Myanmar Judo Association)	15.76 (224 Burmese trainees in Japan; 193 Japanese specialists in Burma)	53.27 [$49.4 million]
2001	0	38.34 (2 debt relief grants); 2.16 (Shan State Kokang Region electrification project); 5.84 (Shan State Kokang Region highway construction equipment); 7.92 (medical equipment for Rangoon hospitals); 2.03 (scholarships for human resource development); 0.35 (equipment for teaching Japanese at the University of Foreign Languages; 3.29 (grass roots projects)[2]	40.8 (621 Burmese trainees in Japan; 342 Burmese exchange students in Japan; 516 Japanese specialists in Burma)	100.73 [$82.9 million]

| 2002 | 0 | 0.76 (1 debt relief grant); 6.28 (Baluchaung #2 hydroelectric plant repair); 4.80 (Dry Zone afforestation project); 6.09 (mother-child healthcare improvement); 2.66 (scholarships for human resources development); 0.03 (equipment for primary school in Insein Township, Rangoon); 0.10 (child health/nutrition project); 0.10 (well construction in Kyaukpadaung, Mandalay Division); 0.80 (grass roots projects)[2] | 36.39 (670 Burmese trainees in Japan; 398 Burmese exchange students in Japan; 439 Japanese specialists in Burma) | 58.01 [$46.3 million] |
| 2003 | 0 | 6.62 (mother-child healthcare improvement); 1.59 (scholarships for human resources development); 0.35 (small-scale bridges in Arakan State); 0.09 (Dry Zone well water improvement); 0.15 (HIV/AIDS prevention in Thai-Burma border area); 1.12 (grass roots projects) | 16.58 (162 Burmese trainees in Japan; 142 Japanese specialists in Burma) | 26.5 [$22.9 million] |

Sources:

Japan. Ministry of Economics, Trade and Industry. 2000. Keizai Kyōryoku no Genjō to Mondaiten [Present Condition and Issues in Economic Cooperation]. Tokyo: METI, s.v. Myanmar.

Japan. Ministry of Foreign Affairs. 1995. Waga Kuni no Seifu Kaihatsu Enjo [Japan's Official Development Assistance], v. 2 Kokubetsu jiseki [Country data]. Tokyo: Association for the Promotion of International Cooperation, s.v. Myanmar.

——. 2001 – 2004. Seifu Kaihatsu Enjo (ODA): Kokubetsu Data Bukku [Official Development Assistance: Country Data Book]. Tokyo: Association for the Promotion of International Cooperation, s.v., Myanmar.

[1] US dollar equivalents in brackets, [], based on average annual exchange rates for each year. Yen and dollar figures are rounded.

[2] 'Grass roots projects' are those in which the Japanese government releases funds to non-governmental organizations (NGOs).

[3] Loan for Rangoon airport modernization included in 1997 fiscal year, ends 31 March 1998.

An example of this ambiguity was the set of ODA guidelines adopted by the government of Prime Minister Kaifu Toshiki in the early 1990s. Formally known as the 'Fundamental Principles of ODA' (*Seifu kaihatsu enjo Taikō*), they state that the Japanese government is committed to taking the following four matters into consideration in making decisions about the allocation of aid to specific countries: (1) that environmental issues as well as economic development be considered; (2) that ODA not be used for military purposes or to stir up international conflicts; (3) that full consideration be paid to the recipient country's military spending, procurement of weapons of mass destruction, development and production of missiles, and export/import of weapons; and (4) that full consideration be paid to conditions for the development of democracy, a market economy, and observance of basic human rights in the recipient country.[36]

Sceptics regarded the Fundamental Principles – especially the fourth principle dealing with democratization and human rights – as little more than window-dressing, designed to placate Japan's western allies. Certainly there was minimal evidence to suggest that they were being consistently implemented. The two largest recipients of Japanese ODA, China and Indonesia, both had authoritarian governments and serious human rights problems. Japan had been the first country to resume large-scale aid to China in the wake of the June 1989 Tian'anmen Massacre. The East Timor crisis, including the killing of as many as 180 unarmed demonstrators by the army outside a Timorese Catholic church in November 1991, had minimal impact on the flow of aid funds between Tokyo and Jakarta, as did the Soeharto regime's suppression of unrest in the mid-1990s.

It was unclear how the four guidelines were to be applied to specific cases. At a symposium on the Burma crisis organized by the Japan branch of Amnesty International, this point was raised by one of the participants, an official of the foreign ministry. He stressed:

> Although the Fundamental Principles of ODA have four points, these are not necessarily a 'negative checklist'. Should [a recipient country] not meet one criterion, this doesn't mean that ODA will be stopped. Rather, a decision is made comprehensively, taking all factors into consideration.[37]

If the Fundamental Principles are interpreted very liberally, the SLORC's original economic liberalization policies in 1988–1989 constituted a reason to continue *some* form of ODA engagement. Such incentives, Japanese government spokesmen argued, would encourage the SLORC to move toward a free market economy. But for the reasons discussed above, this was *not* happening. Moreover, the SLORC's convening of a National Convention in January 1993 to draft a new constitution was understood by some Japanese officials as reflecting the junta's sincere intention of allowing a transfer to civilian rule. According to one U.S. State Department official, a major difference in Tokyo's and Washington's views on Burma was their evaluation of the National Convention: the former tended to take it seriously, while the latter, agreeing with Daw Suu Kyi, regarded it as a sham.[38] But as of early 2006, the drafting process for a new constitution has not been completed.[39]

The SLORC/SPDC clearly fails the standard on military spending: its defence expenditure is, in terms of total government budgets, one of the largest in the world. By the mid-1990s, despite the signing of cease-fires with most of the major border area insurgent groups, the country's army was the second largest in terms of personnel in Southeast Asia, exceeded only by war-battered Vietnam. As the rampant clear cutting of teak forests and over-fishing in Burmese waters indicates, the junta is also minimally concerned with protecting the country's environment.

In 1994, however, it appeared that the SLORC's attitude toward Daw Suu Kyi was softening. In February of that year, it allowed a United States Congressman, Bill Richardson, to meet with her. In September and October, she held two meetings with junta leaders. To reward the SLORC for these gestures, the Japanese government announced in late 1994 that it would approve US$10 to $20 million in new humanitarian aid.[40] In March 1995, the Ministry of International Trade and Industry quietly restored financial risk guarantees for Japanese companies investing in Burma, a decision that could be interpreted as a positive incentive for economic engagement, since the companies would be reimbursed for certain losses incurred while operating in the country.[41] The same month, the government announced a new grant, amounting to ¥1 billion (US$10 million at US$1=¥100), to be used to increase food production in Burma's border areas. This was the largest amount of *new* aid allocated since 1988. According to foreign minister Kono Yōhei, 'We decided on the grant as humanitarian assistance. Therefore, there is no change in our aid policy.' *The Japan Times* in a March 1995 article also quoted Kono as saying, however, that 'Japan hopes that the military junta will take the aid as Tokyo's political message that Tokyo wants to see improvements in human rights in Myanmar.'[42]

Aung San Suu Kyi's release from house arrest on 10 July 1995 represented the high point in 'quiet dialogue'. Japan was the first foreign government to be informed of her release, which, in the words of Bertil Lintner, 'seems to indicate that Tokyo must have played an important behind-the-scenes role in the whole affair'.[43] As in February 1989 when the SLORC announced a schedule for holding elections and Japan normalized relations, it seemed in the summer of 1995 that a political accommodation was within reach.

In October 1995, the Japanese foreign ministry announced the approval of a sum of ¥1.6 billion for renovation of the Institute of Nursing in Rangoon, which it linked to 'such moves toward democratization in Myanmar as the release of Aung San Suu Kyi'.[44] During 30 October–8 November 1995, General Maung Aye, deputy chairman of the SLORC, paid a low profile visit to Japan on his way back from the United Nations General Assembly meeting in New York. He and economic planning minister David Abel visited companies and conferred with Japanese foreign ministry staff on future ODA funding.[45] Now that Daw Suu Kyi was free, the SLORC must have had high expectations that a full reopening of ODA was imminent. However, Tokyo remained cautious. According to a foreign affairs ministry statement issued in July 1995:

In the past, Japanese economic cooperation for Myanmar was virtually halted, with certain exceptions. In view of the progress of the general situation of that country, which was exemplified by the July 1995 lifting of the house arrest imposed on Aung San Suu Kyi, Japan has conducted a partial review of this policy. While closely observing the degree to which democratization progresses, and human rights situation [*sic*] improves, Japan will consider, for the time being, both those projects which are underway, and those projects in the basic human needs sector, which are directly linked to improving the welfare of the people, on case-by-case bases, and will make decisions in the light of its observations as to whether or not to implement these projects.[46]

But democratization after Daw Suu Kyi's release in July 1995 did *not* progress. She was unable to engage the military leadership in negotiations leading to a resolution of the political crisis, and the SLORC did not let up on suppressing the NLD. Foreign countries, including Japan, could do little to stem the confrontation that emerged between the two sides as the decade wore on.

Accusations of 'Suu Kyi bashing' aside, some observers, including the Japanese writers mentioned above, claimed that the responsibility for the bitter political stalemate that continued until she was again put under house arrest in September 2000 rested largely, if not solely, with her. Her first mistake, they argue, was pulling the NLD out of the National Convention in November 1995, protesting its undemocratic nature. She opposed ODA and foreign investment, claiming that foreign capital helped the junta but not the people. One of the targets of her criticism was Japan. In an April 1996 'Letter from Burma' published in the *Mainichi Shimbun*, titled 'Businessmen can only reap what they sow', she wrote:

> To observe businessmen who come to Burma with the intention of enriching themselves is somewhat like watching passers-by in an orchard roughly stripping off blossoms for their fragile beauty, blind to the ugliness of despoiled branches, oblivious of the fact that by their action they are imperilling future fruitfulness and committing an injustice against the rightful owners of the trees. Among these despoilers are big Japanese companies.[47]

In the same letter, she mentions 'forced labour projects where men, women and children toil away without financial compensation under hard taskmasters in scenes reminiscent of the infamous railway of death [between Thailand and Burma] of the Second World War'.[48] For a country wrestling with its history of wartime aggression in Asia, the comparison was highly sensitive.

In an interview with the magazine *THIS IS Yomiuri*, she expressed her opposition to humanitarian aid from Japan, including renovation of the Institute of Nursing:

> *Interviewer*: Let's talk about Japanese aid. Before my coming [to Burma], in discussions with various persons, it became apparent that the Japanese foreign ministry is taking the approach of neither resuming full-scale aid nor stopping aid completely on the basis of principle. 'Humanitarian aid or aid that will be especially effective in raising the people's livelihood will be undertaken on a case-by-case basis. But', they said, 'it is difficult to support the programmes Daw Suu Kyi absolutely opposes.'

> *Suu Kyi*: The reason I clearly and absolutely oppose them is that I don't think they are effective in improving the people's livelihood ... One of these ODA programmes is construction of new facilities for the nursing college. This will not benefit the people as a whole. Those who will secure contracts for construction of the facilities are people with close ties to the regime. They'll make a lot of money on the contracts. Those who will be chosen to attend the school will also be those with connections to the junta. There is no concern that in future these people will work to benefit Burmese people as a whole. To get money, they may work in a private hospital, or go overseas.[49]

Her uncompromising stance on economic engagement, including advocacy of an international boycott of 'Visit Myanmar Year', the 1996–1997 campaign to promote Burma's tourism sector, aroused the generals' bitter resentment. SLORC/SPDC Chairman Than Shwe nurtured a strong animosity against Daw Suu Kyi, which may explain in part the increasingly harsh treatment she received at SPDC hands in the late 1990s – including a November 1996 attack on her motorcade in Rangoon by a mob belonging to the regime's mass organisation, the Union Solidarity Development Association (USDA), which was under Than Shwe's patronage.[50]

Critics sometimes compared her unfavourably to her ideal, Mahatma Gandhi, saying that while Gandhi was a canny politician as well as a saint, the hopelessly idealistic Suu Kyi had no appreciation of the give-and-take of politics. But it was also true that Gandhi and Daw Suu Kyi had radically different opponents. The British authorities in India could be ruthless in suppressing opposition to colonial rule, but they were responsible to Parliament and democratic public opinion at home, and to the rule of law. The SLORC was essentially lawless (in Saw Maung's apt words, 'martial law is no law at all') and determined to wield a power monopoly. So much of the energy and resources of Daw Suu Kyi and her NLD supporters were absorbed in the struggle for survival, including responding to arrests and bullying at the hands of the USDA, that conducting politics in any normal sense was impossible. It should be remembered that at no time, even under extreme provocation, did she abandon her commitment to non-violence.

Moreover, the fundamental issue between Suu Kyi and the SLORC was not ODA or 'Visit Myanmar Year', but conflicting claims to *legitimacy*. She claimed to be the leader of the party which had won the right to form a government in the 1990 election. They saw her as the pawn (the 'axe handle', in their words) of neo-colonialist powers, especially the United States and Britain. The conflict between her and the junta was rooted in perspectives that were basically irreconcilable.

In May 1996, the SLORC began detaining NLD parliamentarians elected in 1990 in order to prevent them from holding a party convention on the sixth anniversary of the ballot. On 22 May, after the first arrests, Japanese Prime Minister Hashimoto Ryūtarō said that they 'were going against the democratization process' and that 'I am closely following developments'.[51] As the arrests continued, chief cabinet secretary Kajiyama Seiroku issued statements that amounted to careful fence sitting: the government was not considering suspending its small-scale humanitarian projects 'because suspending these ongoing projects would damage the people's daily lives'.[52] But when a Japanese newspaper reported in June that the junta was preparing to arrest Aung San Suu Kyi,

Kajiyama stated: 'If [Suu Kyi] is arrested, the government should do more than just call on the Burmese [Myanmar] government for moderation.'[53]

In early 1996, the Japanese government had apparently come close to a consensus on releasing funds allocated for the Mingaladon Airport modernization project. But SLORC's May crackdown on the NLD led these agencies to postpone restarting the project.[54]

Even during the crisis in mid-1996, however, the signals from Japan were mixed. On 24 May, All Nippon Airways presented a petition to the Ministry of Transport to open its direct flight between Kansai and Rangoon.[55] The petition was accepted and, as mentioned above, ANA began its flights in July. Approval of the air route was a small but symbolically important move; given the tense atmosphere in Burma it is surprising that the transport ministry did not delay its decision on ANA's request. On 28 May, Keidanren announced that it was upgrading its informal study group to the 'Japan–Myanmar Economic Committee', a decision which, a Keidanren official admitted, was badly timed, but 'there's no turning back'.[56] Business interests, closely linked to the government, clearly wanted to send the message that 'economics first', the de-linkage of economic engagement and political issues, was alive and well.

On 14 June 1996, Aung San Suu Kyi sent a letter to Prime Minister Hashimoto through the Japanese embassy in Rangoon. She thanked the prime minister and the foreign minister for their support following the SLORC crackdown, and asked that Japan, in concert with other members of international society, use its economic influence to actively promote democratization. This was, she mentioned, one of the Fundamental Principles of ODA adopted by the Japanese government. Prime Minister Hashimoto did not send a reply.[57]

FROM MINGALADON TO DEPAYIN, 1998–2003

On 25 February 1998, a few months shy of the tenth anniversary of the SLORC's bloody power seizure, the Japanese government announced a loan of yen 2.5 billion (US$19.8 million at the prevailing exchange rate) for the renovation of Rangoon's airport, principally improvements to the runway and control tower. As mentioned, airport modernization was the largest single yen loan project in Burma.[58]

It was not clear whether this was a *new* loan, or part of the sum allocated in the 1980s. Moreover, the Japanese government claimed that it was 'humanitarian aid', since, in the words of Asakai Kazuo, Japan's newly appointed ambassador to Rangoon, in an interview with *The Japan Times*: 'The annual number of passengers who use the airport has risen to 1.6 million from 300,000 in 1988... Japan is trying to ensure airport safety with the planned loans from a humanitarian viewpoint. It would be too late if a tragic accident happened.'[59]

But the humanitarian label raised many questions. 'Humanitarian aid' (*jindōteki enjo*) such as the provision of food and medical supplies to help people affected by war or natural catastrophe is usually in the form of grants, not loans, and is generally considered in a separate category from funds used for infrastructure projects. The label might be more meaningful if repair of the airport was necessary to convey food and medical supplies to stricken populations, but most of the people who use Mingaladon are foreign tourists and business people, and a small number of affluent Burmese.

Since All Nippon Airways was operating direct flights between Kansai and Mingaladon in the late 1990s, there was good reason to believe that the Japanese government was under considerable pressure from business interests to do something to lessen the possibility that an ANA jet might crash. Before Ne Win overthrew the elected government of Prime Minister U Nu in March 1962, Mingaladon had been one of Asia's more modern facilities. Three-and-a-half decades later, it was ramshackle and obsolete. Had such a tragedy occurred, Prime Minister Hashimoto might have found himself in the very uncomfortable position of having to answer the charge that moral support for Daw Suu Kyi (the loan freeze) had taken precedence over the safety of Japanese nationals.

But the loan, new or otherwise (and this remains unclear), did serious damage to the credibility of Japan's Burma policy. According to David Arnott, an activist based in Europe:

> Japan has guidelines which prohibit ODA loans to countries which lack democracy and human rights, economic liberalization and environmental sensitivity, and which engage in high military spending. Burma is over-whelmingly disqualified in all these areas, but 'humanitarian' grants can be given with fewer restrictions. The trick is therefore to present the work on the [airport] runway as 'humanitarian' to get round the guidelines.[60]

Although Ambassador Asakai downplayed the differences between Tokyo and Washington on the issue, the United States government had opposed Japan's giving ¥7 billion for the project in summer of 1997.[61] A State Department spokesman, James Foley, commented that the United States 'does not support the resumption of large-scale aid projects in Burma ... at this time'.[62]

In another of her 'Letters from Burma', Daw Suu Kyi criticized the airport loan in no uncertain terms:

> The Japanese government has now decided to provide a substantial sum of money toward repairs to the international airport at Rangoon. It was explained that this sum is a mere fraction of the original amount earmarked for Burma before the troubles of 1988 and that the intended repairs were essential for the maintenance of basic safety for landing aircraft. However, I understand that ICAO [the International Civil Aviation Organisation] is of the opinion that the safety features for which the Japanese money will be used are not essential. This makes the decision of the Japanese government difficult to understand... The resumption of aid in any form will doubtless be used by those with vested interests to claim that there has been an improvement in the human rights record in Burma. In view of the recent wave of arrests, the continuing inhumane treatment of prisoners, the unrelenting repression of political activities and the plight of our refugees and internally displaced persons, the decision of the Japanese government is deeply disappointing.[63]

What made the loan decision especially difficult to understand was that it was made at a time when Japan was suffering from chronic recession and ODA budgets were being cut. However, one major factor seems to have been *Nichibei Myanmā Masatsu* ('Japan–US friction over Myanmar'). *The Irrawaddy* magazine quoted Keio University professor Kusano Atsushi, who had been critical of Daw Suu Kyi's heroic image, complaining that 'Tokyo is always concerned about how the United States will react. But the United States and European nations have invested far more in Myanmar than Japan has over the past five years.' He recommended 'a more pragmatic approach' in order to prevent markets from being lost to Japanese companies. *The Irrawaddy's* commentator suggested that 'Always eager to open Japan's markets, the United States has made it clear that the best thing Japan can do for the rest of Asia is to put its own house in order and increase domestic demand for foreign goods and services. Thus Japan, perhaps tired of being told to behave like a good housewife whose place is in the home, has shown signs of succumbing to the flattering attentions of governments eager for access to purse-strings significantly looser than those of the IMF.'[64]

In 1999 and 2000, the prospects for political reconciliation seemed more remote than ever. Reacting to the NLD's establishment of a 'Committee Representing the People's Parliament' in September 1998, in effect creating a parallel government composed of elected members of parliament, the SPDC detained hundreds of MPs and party leaders, forced tens of thousands of ordinary members to resign, and closed down NLD branches. The USDA, which at the time comprised as much as forty per cent of the adult population, held mass rallies nationwide expressing 'no confidence' in NLD parliamentarians, and demanding that the party be banned. The regime's newspaper, the *Myanma Alin* (*New Light of Myanmar*), published crude cartoons of the pro-democracy leader as a gap-toothed old hag, salivating with power-lust while she watches Myanmar marching triumphantly to developed nationhood.

But the regime's most vicious attack on her occurred when it turned down her husband Michael Aris's request for a visa. He

Burmese Refugees in Japan

Following the SLORC's 1988 power seizure, thousands of student activists and others who had supported the pro-democracy movement left central Burma. Many of them went to the border areas to carry on armed resistance, while others began an insecure life as exiles in neighbouring countries, especially Thailand. In mid-1991, Bertil Lintner wrote in an article for the *Far Eastern Economic Review* that as many as 10,000 young Burmese had made their way to Tokyo, where they struggled to survive as manual laborers, most of them working in bars or restaurants, while smaller groups lived in Osaka, Nagoya and other cities. Attracted by the availability of jobs in the service sector and, according to Lintner, the 'leniency' of the Japanese authorities, who were reluctant to send them back to Burma, their situation nonetheless remained fundamentally insecure: even though the Japanese government did not attempt to round up and deport them, it was almost impossible for them to gain formal recognition as refugees, which would have given them legal protection. By 1991, only one Burmese couple had been granted this status. Although Japan has signed the 1951 United Nations convention on refugees, the process of obtaining refugee status was lengthy, complicated and bureaucratically ambiguous, especially compared to procedures in western countries (Lintner, 1991: 28, 29).

The situation was fundamentally unchanged in 2005. According to statistics compiled by the People's Forum on Burma, a Japanese citizens' group that has aided Burmese in their attempts to gain recognized refugee status, there were 367 applications for such status from Burmese people in Japan between 1992 and 2004, of which 61 were successful, while 89 other applicants had been given 'special permits' apparently enabling them to stay until their applications were processed (People's Forum on Burma, 2004). The total number, 150 (including those on special permits), was small compared to the number of potential applicants among Burmese in Japan (estimated at around 10,000 in 2002), reflecting the strictness of Japan's policy on refugees and immigrants in general (Lawrence, 2002). But Burmese constituted 14 of 15 persons granted refugee status by the Ministry of Justice in 2004 (*The Japan Times*, 2005).

The Japanese government's apparent 'tilt' in favour of Burmese applicants did not reflect explicit policy, but a bureaucratic bias influenced by domestic civil society and government agency lobbying, largely behind the scenes. This in turn illustrated a fundamental problem with Japanese policy-making: its ambiguity and non-transparency.

was dying from cancer and wanted to spend his last days with her in Rangoon. The SPDC apparently saw this personal tragedy as an opportunity to get her out of their hair, recommending that she go to Britain to see him. Reluctant to do so since she might not be allowed to return to Burma, she was even denied the chance to talk to him over the telephone, since Rangoon operators frequently disconnected the line. Dr. Aris died on 27 March 1999, coincidentally Armed Forces (or Anti-Fascist Resistance) Day. According to diplomatic sources in Rangoon, the SPDC's insensitivity was something even she, who had been struggling with them almost single-handedly since 1988, had not expected.[65]

'Quiet dialogue' between Rangoon and Tokyo continued, despite the intensifying hard line. In January of 1999, Brigadier Kyaw Win, a close subordinate of Lieutenant General Khin Nyunt, director of military intelligence, visited the Japanese capital with three other intelligence officers to talk with foreign ministry officials, members of the Diet and businessmen. At a Tokyo news conference, one of the delegation members, Lieutenant-Colonel Hla Min, mentioned that a general election would be held in two or three years, following the National Convention's drafting of the new constitution. In November of that year, Prime Minister Obuchi Keizō met with SPDC Chairman Than Shwe at the ASEAN Summit in Manila. The first Japanese prime minister to meet with a Burmese leader in fifteen years, Obuchi stressed the importance of starting dialogue with the opposition. But former Prime Minister Hashimoto, leading an unofficial delegation to Rangoon following the summit, criticized the sanctions policies of the United States and the European Union, claiming that they 'drive the Burmese leadership into a corner and make it more and more obstinate'.[66] Significantly, his delegation's four-day visit was sponsored by an influential Japanese non-governmental organization, the Sasagawa Peace Foundation, which was becoming a key player in efforts to promote economic and other forms of engagement with the SPDC.

By the end of 2000, Daw Suu Kyi was back under house arrest, having been detained after trying to board a train to Mandalay in order to meet with local NLD members.[67] But hope for resolution of the political crisis came from a new quarter: United Nations Secretary General Kofi Annan's special envoy to Burma Razali Ismail. The Malaysian diplomat carried out intense shuttle diplomacy to get the dialogue process started, announcing in January 2001 that Daw Suu Kyi had begun secret talks with SPDC leaders. Pro-democracy Burmese abroad and foreign governments were guardedly optimistic: the All Burma Students Democratic Front, a major dissident organisation based in Thailand, described the talks as 'the most positive sign we've seen since the general election held in May 1990'.[68]

Shortly before Razali made his momentous announcement, the right-wing *Sankei Shimbun* newspaper published an article reporting that a team of specialists had been sent by the Japan International Cooperation Agency (JICA) to inspect the Baluchaung hydro-electric station in early 2000. The team reported that the facility was in a terrible state of disrepair, and that extensive renovations were necessary to keep the station, which provides Burma with about thirty per cent of its electric power, operable. *Sankei* also reported that Yugoslavia had offered aid, the sum of US$30 million, to SPDC Chairman Than Shwe for this purpose, and that it was highly likely that the real origin of the funds was China, which was using its close ally Yugoslavia to funnel the funds into Burma. The article, published in a paper known for its strong antagonism to China, also expressed the suspicion that Beijing was actually using recycled funds that it had received from Japan as ODA to promote its own national interests inside Burma, while Japan's interests were hobbled by considerations of democracy and human rights.[69]

Sankei's allegation about China's misuse of Tokyo's ODA funds could not be verified, and a spokesman for the Japanese government, responding to a question from a member of the House of Representatives of the Diet, said that 'Companies involved in a contract for a specific project approved by the Japanese government will be paid in accordance with the contract of concern, therefore making it impossible for funds to be used for other purposes in a third country'.[70] But from Japan's perspective China was emerging in the early twenty-first century as both an opportunity and a threat, and Beijing's dominant influence in Burma – eclipsing that of Japan – was increasingly a source of concern.

In April 2001, Tokyo announced that it would provide yen 3.5 billion (US\$28 million) in grant funds for the repair of the plant. Like the airport renovation, this was described as 'humanitarian aid', again arousing international criticism. President George W. Bush's secretary of state, Colin Powell, testified before the US Senate that the funds 'were not a proper investment to be making at this time, with this regime'.[71] In a 28 April 2001 article published in the *International Herald Tribune*, Burma specialist David I. Steinberg, a prominent and rather moderate figure in the ongoing debate about 'constructive engagement', argued that just as in the 1970s and 1980s, when ODA funds flowed from Tokyo to Rangoon without 'conditionality', so 'the Japanese may be sending too strong a signal, too early, to the Burmese authorities' by approving the Baluchaung grant.[72]

On 6 May 2002, Aung San Suu Kyi was released from her second term of house arrest. But hopes that reconciliation between her and the junta could be achieved were again disappointed. She began a series of upcountry tours to strengthen NLD organization and leadership, including one to Mandalay Division in June that was characterized by generally cooperative relations between her people and local SPDC authorities. But on subsequent trips, tensions mounted. It appears the top leadership was deeply shocked by her continued nationwide popularity. Despite the fact that she had been largely confined to Rangoon since 1989, the junta had not succeeded in marginalizing her. There was a tremendous potential for popular unrest, fuelled by inflation and chronic economic insecurity. In defiance of official warnings, tens of thousands of ordinary people came out to see her.

On 30 May 2003, while returning from Kachin State, she and her entourage were attacked near the town of Depayin in Sagaing Division by a gang armed with bamboo staves and swords who killed as many as 70 or 80 of her people. Although the junta claimed that the violence had been provoked by the NLD, other witnesses said the gang, made up of USDA members and even freed convicts, had ambushed them. There was evidence to suggest that the incident had been sanctioned at least implicitly on the highest levels of the SPDC leadership.[73]

In July, US President George Bush signed into law a tough new set of sanctions, the 'Burmese Freedom and Democracy Act', which banned financial transactions with Burmese parties and exports to the United States from the country. That same month, Foreign Minister Kawaguchi Yoriko expressed disappointment that the SPDC had not responded to Tokyo's concerns about Daw Suu Kyi, whom it was keeping incommunicado after the 30 May incident, saying that 'We cannot continue as if nothing has happened... Under the current situation, we have no choice but to put off new aid.'[74] Yet as in the past, it was difficult to interpret what this meant. That there would be no new yen loans? But these had been frozen, with the possible exception of the 1998 airport funds, since 1988. Or that grants and genuine humanitarian aid would also be cut off? This seemed to be true after Kawaguchi's July statement, but by October 2003, the flow of such grants – including 'grassroots assistance' given to non-governmental organisations – had resumed.[75] In July 2004, more than a year after Black Friday, Tokyo announced a new grant of ¥3.4 billion (US$30.9) for reforestation projects in the Dry Zone of central Burma.[76] Yet Daw Suu Kyi remained under house arrest, virtually in solitary confinement, and a resolution of Burma's political crisis seemed more unattainable than ever.

NOTES

[1] *Asahi Shimbun* (1998b). At the time, the new league had about 30 LDP Dietmen as members.

[2] Tokyo Broadcasting System (1994); *Dawn* (1990: 13).

[3] Burma Action Group (1996: 44).

[4] Comments of Japanese Burma specialist to author, Tokyo, 26-28 February 1992.

5   Ibid.

6   *Bangkok Post* (1990).

7   According to an official at the United States embassy in Rangoon interviewed by this writer in March 1991, the SLORC's naïve generals mistook Daichi for the Daiichi Kangyō Bank, formerly Japan's largest bank, and leapt at the opportunity to link up to this financial powerhouse. MCDO's office was in the New Otani Business Centre, and according to centre staff was closed in late 1991 or early 1992.

8   According to Wai Phyo Myint (2004), 200 second-hand Japanese buses were ordered for use in Rangoon in 2004.

9   Sender (1996: 48).

10 TBS (1994); *Myanmaa Nyusu* [Myanmar News] (1994: 11-20).

11 *Mainichi Daily News* (1996).

12 *Far Eastern Economic Review* (1994a: 65).

13 *Ryukyu Shimpo* (1996). By the late 1990s, seven Japanese banks had offices in Rangoon.

14 Sender (1996: 48).

15 *Asahi Shimbun* (1996); Economist Intelligence Unit (1996: 19); *The Irrawaddy* (1998a).

16 Earthrights International (2000: 13).

17 Nagai (1997: 300-02).

18 Ibid.

19 Ohmae (1997b: 5).

20 Ohmae (1997).

21 Ibid.

22 Ibid.

23 Ohmae (1997a).

24 Steinberg (2001: 153, 154); Chinese investment is unlisted, but probably bigger if border business is included. The size of the American figure is due in part to oil company Unocal's partnership in the Yadana Pipeline Project.

25 *The Irrawaddy* (1998a).

26 Toriumi (1998: 2, 3).

27 *Ryūkyū Shimpo* (2000).

28   Kyodo (2002). The reason for the ban was to protect Burmese trading companies, which were running out of hard currency.

29   Matthews (2001: 231).

30   Annual revenues from the Yadana natural gas field to the SPDC have been estimated to be as high as US$400 million a year.

31   *The Japan Times* (1992).

32   *The Japan Times* (1995a).

33   *Asahi Shimbun* (1996b); Japan. Ministry of Foreign Affairs, vol. 2 (1995: 156, 157).

34   Japan Network on Debt and Poverty (2003).

35   Ibid.

36   Japan. Ministry of Foreign Affairs, vol. 1 (1995: 46-51).

37   Amnesty International-Japan Branch (1995: 69).

38   Comment of U.S. State Department official to author, Washington, 28 April 1994.

39   The National Convention was re-convened in May 2004, but had not produced a constitutional draft by early 2006.

40   *Far Eastern Economic Review* (1994b).

41   *Far Eastern Economic Review* (1995).

42   *The Japan Times* (1995).

43   Lintner (1995: 15).

44   Japan. Ministry of Foreign Affairs (1995a); Masaki (1995: 3).

45   Masaki (1995a); *Myanmaa Nyusu* (1995-96: 4, 5).

46   Quote by official, Japan Ministry of Foreign Affairs, to author, in correspondence dated 11 June 1996.

47   Aung San Suu Kyi (1996a: 3).

48   Ibid.

49   *THIS IS Yomiuri* (1996: 204, 205).

50   According to an informant who talked with this writer in Rangoon in 2003 and 2004, General Than Shwe, the embodiment of traditional Burmese male values, found the stubborn, straight-talking Daw Suu Kyi insufferable, and the conflict between them had a strong personal dimension.

51 *Daily Yomiuri* (1996).

52 *The Japan Times* (1996).

53 *Mainichi Daily News* (1996a).

54 *Asahi Shimbun* (1996b).

55 *Asahi Shimbun* (1996a).

56 *Mainichi Daily News* (1996).

57 *Asahi Shimbun* (1996c).

58 *Asahi Shimbun* (1998); formal notification of the loan was given on 11 March 1998, which was in the 1997 fiscal year. See *Asahi Shimbun* (1998a).

59 Masaki (1998).

60 David Arnott (1988).

61 *Ryūkyū Shimpo* (1997).

62 Masaki (1998).

63 Aung San Suu Kyi (1998).

64 *The Irrawaddy* (1998).

65 Seekins (2000: 18-20).

66 Wingfield (2000: 211).

67 Matthews (2001: 236).

68 Lintner (2001: 22).

69 *Sankei Shimbun* (2000).

70 'Japanese Grant for Repair of Baluchaung Hydropower Plant II' (2001). In other words, the Chinese government would never, at any stage of the ODA process, have access to the funds.

71 Reuters News Agency (2001).

72 Steinberg (2001a).

73 The most complete account of what became known as 'Black Friday' was published by the Alternative ASEAN Network on Burma (ALTSEAN, 2003).

74 Reuters News Agency (2003).

75 Burma Information Network-Japan (2003); Mekong Watch (2004).

76 *Asahi Shimbun* (2004a).

Chapter Six

CONCLUSIONS

'Black Friday' and the hopelessness that ensued after Aung San Suu Kyi was placed under her third term of house arrest seemed to underline the futility of Tokyo's 'quiet dialogue'. But as mentioned in Chapter 4 (pp. 99, 100), this policy, combined with partial restoration of ODA, promised good results when it was adopted in 1989, and even when Daw Suu Kyi was first released from house arrest in 1995. But Japanese policymakers who were committed to promoting political and economic reform in Burma seem to have made a number of crucial miscalculations that were conditioned by widely held perceptions of how Asia was changing at the end of the Cold War.

First, from the precedent of countries like South Korea, Taiwan and Thailand, it was assumed that democratization and the growth of a 'civil society' sustained by an expanding and politically aware middle class were irreversible trends. Factors specific to Burma – its geo-strategic vulnerability, a turbulent history of inter-ethnic relations and the violent collision between *Tatmadaw*-based authoritarianism and a tradition of revolutionary nationalism going back at least to Aung San – were imperfectly understood.

Thailand and Burma share common cultural and religious values, especially Theravada Buddhism; but politically and socially they are strikingly divergent. Under a stable constitutional monarchy, Thailand has opened up to the outside world. Deeply influenced by international values, its society has become more diverse and contentious, especially since the 1980s.[1] But Burma has followed a trajectory that seems more typical of many African countries, where economic and social progress has been thwarted not only by unmitigated ethnic antagonisms, but also by élites who have grossly mismanaged African economies and have used the export of natural resources as a cash cow.[2] The case of Burma shows the danger of making simple-minded assumptions about 'culture' – e.g., that since Thailand, Burma and neighbouring Asian countries share 'common cultural values', their development will be essentially the same, with only small local variations. The issue is not culture, but different *power equations* within the different countries.

Secondly, few observers in the late 1980s could have predicted China's rapid emergence as an economic and military power in the Asian region, or its aggressive strategies of engagement with the SLORC. Although it may be an exaggeration to say that Burma has become a Chinese satellite (or neo-colony), the influence of Beijing has eclipsed that of Tokyo. As mentioned in Chapter 5, dependable Chinese economic and moral support has given the SPDC the luxury of being able to ignore international criticism over its human rights record. In the words of one Burmese observer, 'As long as China remains friendly nothing will change. China can provide everything the country needs from a needle to a nuclear bomb.'[3] After Black Friday, even Malaysia's Prime Minister Mahathir, a close friend of the junta and sponsor of its entry into ASEAN, criticised the SPDC's intransigence; but Beijing offered it unwavering moral support.

Thirdly, the Japanese and western governments over-estimated the extent to which *economic incentives* could influence the behaviour of the junta. The implied promise of generous ODA from Tokyo and the disincentive of western sanctions both were based on the assumption that the SLORC/SPDC felt a desperate need for foreign capital and that once they calculated the economic benefits for themselves, they would be willing to concede political space to Daw Suu Kyi, the NLD and ethnic minorities. But although individual generals have often been corrupt, economic self-interest has never taken priority over their top goal, which is to enforce an unchallenged monopoly of power inside the country.

The fundamental and probably unshakeable beliefs of the SPDC, like the pre-1997 SLORC, are that: (1) Burma is a 'racially' homogeneous nation, whose ethnic divisions are the work of foreign colonialists and neo-colonialists; as was mentioned in Chapter One, the concept of a *Maha Bama* ('Greater Burma') Nation was exploited by wartime leader Ba Maw; (2) to defend national independence and sovereignty, Burma must have a strong and unified state; and (3) this state in the final analysis must be controlled in a top-down fashion by the *Tatmadaw*, even if 'democratic' parties are given a façade role. SPDC Chairman Than Shwe has shown in recent years an increasing willingness to sacrifice economic internationalization to maintain the army's – and his own – power monopoly. Foreign private investment has plunged since the late 1990s, but the regime survives. And the backing of China and ASEAN combined with exports of raw materials like natural gas makes a reverse course to a non-liberal and state-dominated economy relatively pain-free for the military élite and their cronies, though not for ordinary Burmese.

A final miscalculation shared by many Japanese and other observers was that the SLORC was composed of poorly-educated and dim-witted 'men in trousers' who, through their ineptness in running the country would either be overthrown from without by the people, or from within by a 'reformist' movement of officers on the model of the 1986 'People's Power' Revolution in the Philippines. While some Japanese foreign ministry officials watched carefully for frictions between 'hard liners' and 'reformists' in the junta, they underestimated both its unity and its canny survival skills. This was true not only in the 1988–1990 period, when foreign exchange coffers were almost empty and the SLORC was desperate for cash, but in 1997 when the State Law and Order Restoration Council was re-organised as the State Peace and Development Council. This was a delicate operation, involving the purge of generals who were known to be corrupt and their replacement in most cases by younger officers. The three top leaders – Than Shwe, Maung Aye and Khin Nyunt – remained in place, and a long-anticipated split in the *Tatmadaw* did not occur. Khin Nyunt's purge in October

2004 showed again that while even top military figures were expendable, the *Tatmadaw* had achieved a durable state of 'system maintenance'.

It is very difficult to say whether some alternative to 'quiet diplomacy' would have been more effective in influencing the junta's behaviour. Japan could have adopted a consistent hard line policy like the West, refusing to concede government-to-government recognition to the SLORC and holding back *all* aid, not just yen loan disbursements. But there were big risks, which may have become apparent to Tokyo when the junta began its anti-Japanese campaign in the media at the time of Ogata Sadako's 1990 human rights mission: that the new generation of military leaders, whose emotional ties to Japan are rather weak, would seek more cooperative partners elsewhere in Asia. The opposite alternative, full economic engagement on the pre-1988 model, would have aroused the opposition of Japan's major trade and security partner, the United States. To minimise risk and unpredictability in a country perceived by policymakers as playing a major role in Japan's national interest, a middle way had to be found.

Japan's Burma policy has been criticized – by no less than Aung San Suu Kyi herself – as mercenary, putting economic interests above human rights. Yet the majority of post-1988 aid has been in the form of humanitarian and debt relief grants (the latter constituting no real financial gain for the SLORC/SPDC). In this writer's opinion, there is no reason why humanitarian aid should *not* be given, even if some of it benefits the regime. Burma is in such bad shape in terms of food security and health (including one of Asia's biggest AIDS epidemics) that opposing such aid – as supporters of western sanctions do – does more harm than good. It should be apparent by now that while Burma's democratization remains a *long-term* goal of the international community, humanitarian needs are desperate and immediate.

In the wake of Black Friday, U.S. President George W. Bush signed the 'Burmese Freedom and Democracy Act' into law. At the time, this was celebrated by his administration as an example of American 'moral' foreign policy at work, but it soon became apparent that the harsh sanctions were hitting the wrong targets. The embargo on Burmese imports to the United States put tens of thousands of women who worked in export-oriented textile factories out of a job, and many were forced for lack of alternatives to enter Burma's burgeoning sex industry.[4] Moreover, President Bush's initiative did *not* affect the participation of Unocal, a politically well-connected American oil company, in the notorious Yadana Pipeline Project.[5] While the shuttered textile factories generated only a few million dollars annually in export revenues, the Yadana and Yetagun projects net the SPDC several hundred million dollars a year, and provide few if any employment opportunities for ordinary Burmese. Indeed, as mentioned in Chapter 5, the pipeline projects have resulted in *Tatmadaw*-instigated forced labour and forced relocation for ethnic minorities living in the area. It is difficult to see how such inconsistencies and loopholes on the part of the U.S. government can contribute to Burmese democracy.

Japan's Burma policy is also criticized because of its ambiguity, which reflects a fundamental problem in the Japanese political system: the domination of policy-making by non-elected bureaucrats and politically mobilized special interests who are largely insulated from public and parliamentary scrutiny. The Diet has only occasionally held debates on Burma, and most decision-making on ODA and other matters relating to the country is made behind the scenes. This has made understanding the dynamics of Japanese policymaking on Burma almost as challenging as comprehending the internal dynamics of the SPDC! Thus, there have been 'surprises' like the 1998 airport loan that undermine Japan's credibility with the pro-democracy movement, western nations and international society as a whole.

In other words, the major problem may not be with the Japanese government's aid presence *per se*, but with the way Tokyo has rationalized and explained, or failed to explain, its ODA decisions. Had the government defined its policy in terms of clear-cut principles and adhered to them consistently (as it has *not* adhered in any meaningful way to the 1992 'Fundamental Principles of ODA'), perhaps it could have played a more effective role in developing an international response to the Burma crisis, even if its policy was quite different from that of the United States and other western countries. Genuine commitment to such principles would have sacrificed some flexibility, but 'strategic ambiguity' seems a good example of the common criticism that Japan's foreign policy is *ad hoc* and lacking a coherent philosophy beyond defence of bureaucratic turf and short term self-interest.

In the opening years of the 21st century, Burma–Japan relations are cordial. The flow of ODA grants continues, and – partly in order to minimize international criticism – Tokyo seems to be adopting the stratagem of 'folding' its economic support of the SPDC into a regional context, through providing funds for regional projects such as the Greater Mekong Subregion, of which Burma is a member, and ASEAN-related endeavours.[6]

In December 2003, Prime Minister Koizumi Junichirō sponsored the Japan–ASEAN Summit in Tokyo, and junta-controlled media prominently displayed photographs of Koizumi shaking hands with a business-suited Khin Nyunt. While in Tokyo, the newly appointed prime minister also met with Sasagawa Yōhei, president of the Nippon Foundation and son of the founder of the well-endowed Sasagawa complex of non-governmental organizations. The Sasagawa Peace Foundation's activities in Burma – including economic research, sponsorship of academic conferences and subsidising the *Myanmar Times and Business Weekly*, a glossy English-language alternative to the Stalinist *New Light of Myanmar* – show that governmental restraint in relation to the SPDC need not be matched by the Japanese private sector. Thus, Tokyo's influence in the country is likely to persist, despite China's commanding presence.

In the post-Cold War era, which coincides with Burma's post-1988 political crisis, new spheres of influence and power are being carved out in Asia. Because of historical circumstances and the weakness of Burmese political institutions, the country's military leaders have not found a way to respond positively to external challenges. Burma remains a ground of contention for richer and more powerful states, just as it was when the British occupied Mandalay in 1885 and when the Imperial Japanese Army with its BIA auxiliaries stormed across the Thai border in December 1941.

NOTES

1 Though Thai democrats feared a reverse course during the time when Thaksin Shinawatra was prime minister (2001–2006)

2 According to Ugandan President Yoweri Museveni, 'Burma was much richer than Singapore, but because of wrong policies it is not now. That was the problem we had in Africa. The whole of Africa was "Burmanized" by wrong policies, but now we are "[un]Burmanizing" ourselves.' *The Irrawaddy* (2004). Like Ne Win, Museveni's predecessor, Idi Amin, drove Indian entrepreneurs out of the country.

3 Perlez (2004).

4 Daley (2003).

5 President Clinton's 1997 ban on U.S. investment was non-retroactive, and since the Yadana project was not exporting natural gas to the U.S., the 2003 law did not affect it.

6 *Asahi Shimbun* (2004). See also Jennings (2005): 'Japan's recent $1 million technical assistance grant to upgrade a coastal transit corridor from Vietnam to Thailand looks at first like typical governmental largesse … But to Southeast Asia, the grant indicates again that Japan has strategic economic designs on the five countries that make up the 200-million-strong Mekong basin – Cambodia, Laos, Myanmar, Thailand and Vietnam – according to officials at the Second Greater Mekong Subregion Summit in Kunming, China.'

CHRONOLOGY OF BURMA–JAPAN
RELATIONS, 1940–2004

1940	**May:** Col. Suzuki Keiji arrives in Rangoon. **August:** Aung San leaves for Amoy, China. **November:** Aung San meets Suzuki in Tokyo.
1941	**March:** Aung San returns to Burma to recruit Thirty Comrades: **Mid-year:** Minami Kikan begins training Thirty Comrades on Hainan Island. **8 December:** Pacific War begins. **28 December:** Burma Independence Army (BIA) formally established in Bangkok.
1942	**January:** Japanese forces capture Kawthaung, Tavoy, Mergui and Moulmein. **February:** Japanese cross Sittang River. **March:** Rangoon falls. **April–June:** BIA attacks on Karens (Myaungmya) and Arakanese Muslims. **May:** Mandalay and Lashio captured, Burma Road cut. British end Burma campaign. **June:** Japanese establish provisional Burmese government with Dr. Ba Maw as head. BIA dissolved, replaced by Burma Defence Army (BDA).

1943	**1 August:** Premier Tōjō declares the 'independence' of Burma within the Greater East Asia Co-Prosperity Sphere.
	5–6 November: Greater East Asia Conference in Tokyo, attended by Ba Maw as head of state of Burma (*Adipadi*).
1944	**March–June:** Unsuccessful Imphal Offensive into northeastern India, resulting in as many as 80,000 Japanese casualties.
	August: Aung San and communists establish Anti-Fascist Organization.
	Late 1944: Allied offensives into northern Burma commence.
1945	**27 March:** Aung San leads Burma National Army uprising against Japanese.
	2–3 May: Rangoon recaptured by Allies, including Patriotic Burmese Forces.
	15 August: Japan surrenders.
1946	Takeyama Michio's novel *Biruma no Tategoto* (*Harp of Burma*) published.
1948	**4 January:** Union of Burma achieves independence from British colonial rule.
1952	**28 April:** Allied occupation of Japan ends.
1954	**4 November:** Union of Burma and Japan sign peace treaty, agreement on war reparations (total: US$250 million).
1960	**March:** First phase of Baluchaung hydro-power project completed.
1962	**2 March:** General Ne Win overthrows U Nu government in a coup d'état. Establishes Revolutionary Council and state socialist economy.
1965–1977	Additional Japanese war reparations paid to Burma, totaling US$140 million.
1974	Burma joins the Asia Development Bank.
1976–1977	Japanese aid commitments/disbursements to Burma increase 450%–500% in 1977 compared to 1976.

1985–1986 Aung San Suu Kyi at Centre of Southeast Asian Studies, Kyoto University.

1987 **5 September:** Ne Win orders demonetization without compensation of Burmese bank notes.

11 December: United Nations approves Least Developed Nation (LDC) status for Burma.

1988 **Early 1988:** Aung Gyi, former close associate of Ne Win, meets Japanese businessmen and politicians in Rangoon. They urge economic reforms.

April: U Tin Tun, Burma's deputy prime minister, meets Japanese prime minister and finance minister in Tokyo. They urge fundamental reforms.

March – early September: Massive popular protests in Rangoon and other towns.

13 September: Japanese government announces an ODA 'freeze' due to political instability. **18 September:** State Law and Order Restoration Council (SLORC) seizes power.

28 September: Japanese ambassador Ohtaka states that resumption of ODA flows depends on political stabilization.

1989 **4 January:** Along with other diplomats, Ambassador Ohtaka boycotts SLORC's Independence Day celebrations.

25 January: Nihon–Biruma Kyōkai petitions Japanese government to resume ODA flows.

17 February: Japanese government formally recognizes SLORC. Some committed ODA funds are released, but new funds not committed.

20 July: Aung San Suu Kyi placed under house arrest.

1989–1990 Sale of Burma Embassy land in Tokyo provides SLORC with much-needed hard currency, about US$435 million.

1990 **27 May:** NLD victory in general election.

30 August: Watanabe Michio, leading member of Japan's ruling LDP, visits Rangoon and urges Daw Suu Kyi's release.

November: Ogata Sadako visits Rangoon under UN auspices to inspect human rights conditions. Anti-Japanese campaign begins in the state-run media.

1990–2000 Japan gives debt relief grants totaling ¥64.06 billion (US$544 million).

1991 **October:** Announcement that Daw Suu Kyi has won the Nobel Peace Prize. Japanese officials urge her release from house arrest.

1995 **10 July:** Daw Suu Kyi released from house arrest, behind-the-scenes role of Japan believed to be important factor.

October: Japan announces ¥1.6 billion for renovation of Rangoon Nursing Institute.

1996 Daw Suu Kyi criticizes Japanese ODA and business activities in Burma.

24 May: All Nippon Airways petitions Japanese Government to open direct Kansai– Rangoon flight. **July:** Flights begin.

1998 **28 February:** Japanese government formally announces ¥2.5 billion loan for modernization of Rangoon's airport. Airport loan is labeled 'humanitarian aid'.

2001 **April:** Japanese government announces ¥3.5 billion for repair of Baluchaung hydro-electric plant as dialogue ensues between Daw Suu Kyi and SPDC.

2003 **30 May:** 'Black Friday' incident: SPDC attacks on Daw Suu Kyi and supporters near Depayin, Sagaing Division. Foreign Minister Kawaguchi Yoriko expresses disappointment over incident.

2004 **July:** Japanese government announces ¥3.4 billion for reforestation project in central Burma.

BIBLIOGRAPHY AND REFERENCES

Ajia Chū–Tō Dōkō Nempō [Yearbook of Asia–Middle East Trends]. 1982. Tokyo: Institute of Developing Economies.

Akazu Mizuha. 1994. *Aung San Suu Kyi: Tatakau kujaku* [Aung San Suu Kyi: the Fighting peacock]. Super Nobel Prize Story, vol. 2. Tokyo: Ōtō Shobō.

Allen, Louis. 2000. *Burma: the Longest War.* London: Phoenix Press.

Alternative ASEAN Network on Burma (ALTSEAN). 2003. 'Briefing: Black Friday And the Crackdown on the NLD'. Bangkok, 11 June.

Amnesty International–Japan Branch. 1995. *Biruma jiyū e harukanaru michi* [On the long road to freedom in Burma]. Tokyo: Amnesty International.

Armed Forces Day, 1996 Fifty First Anniversary: Poems, Essays, Stories. 1998. Rangoon: Printing and Publishing Enterprise.

Arnott, David. 1998. 'Japanese ODA and Orwellian logic.' Posted to *Burmanet News* at: burmanet-l@igc.ap.org, 15 March.

Asahi Shimbun. 1992. 'Inochi no mizu, ongaeshi no suidō [The water of life, gratitude's pipeline]'. 12 January.

——. 1996. 'Myanmā de tennen gasu jigyō [Natural gas enterprise in Myanmar]'. 10 April.

——. 1996a. 'Myanmā chōkkō bin seikyū [Petition for a direct flight to Myanmar]'. 25 May.

——. 1996b. 'Machinozomu kigyō ni kata sukashi [Dodging eagerly expectant enterprises]'. 13 June.

——. 1996c. 'Enjo, keizai kyōryoku de Nihon wa eikyōryoku; minshuka e kokusai shakai to tōitsu kōdō o [Japan has strong influence through aid and economic cooperation; together with international society, work to promote democratization]'. 23 July.

——. 1998. 'Tai Myanmā en shakkan o zaikai: nijū-go oku en [Reopening of yen loans to Myanmar: 2.5 billion yen]'. 26 February.

——. 1998a. 'Tai Myanmā en shakkan no saikai: Seifu seishiki ni tsutaeru [Reopening of yen loans to Myanmar: the government makes a formal announcement]'. 12 March.

——. 1998b. 'Jimin ni, Myanmā ōendan [Myanmar fan club in the LDP]'. 5 June.

——. 2003. 'Seijika garami soba tensaku hyōryū [Soba crop substitution caught up in politics]'. 5 September.

——. 2004. 'Mekong ryūiki kaihatsu shien kasoku [Support accelerates for development of the Mekong river basin]'. 9 June.

——. 2004a. 'Myanmā e seifu shien saikai [Government aid to Myanmar is reopened]'. 10 July.

Asian Development Bank. 1991. *Asian Development Outlook, 1991.* Manila: Asian Development Bank.

Atarashii Rekishi Kyōkasho [*New History Textbook*]. 2001. Tokyo: Fusōsha.

Aung San. 1993. 'Burma's Challenge'. In Josef Silverstein (ed.), *The Political Legacy of Aung San.* Rev. ed. Ithaca: Cornell University Southeast Asia Program.

Aung San Suu Kyi. 1991. *Aung San of Burma.* 2nd ed. Edinburgh: Kiscadale.

——. 1991a. *Jiyū* [Freedom]. Translation of *Freedom from Fear* by Yumiko Janson. Tokyo: Shūeisha.

——. 1995. 'Speech to a Mass Rally at the Shwedagon Pagoda.' In Michael Aris (ed.), *Freedom from Fear and Other Writings.* Rev. ed. London: Penguin, pp. 192–98.

——. 1996. *Aung San Suu Kyi Enzetsu Shū* [Collected speeches of Aung San Suu Kyi]. Translated by Ino Kenji. Tokyo: Misuzu Shobō.

——. 1996a. 'Letter from Burma', no. 22. *Mainichi Daily News*, 22 April, p. 3.

——. 1998. 'Letter from Burma: Japan's aid to military junta fuels oppression'. *Mainichi Daily News*, 6 April, p. 2.

Aung Zaw. 2003. 'Burma's Yadaya Battle'. *The Irrawaddy*, vol. 11: 8, October 2003: p. 27.

Aung-Thwin, Michael. 1989. '1948 and Burma's Myth of Independence'. In Josef Silverstein (ed.), *Independent Burma at Forty Years: Six Assessments*. Ithaca: Cornell University Southeast Asia Program: pp. 19–34.

Ba Maw. 1968. *Breakthrough in Burma: Memoirs of a Revolution, 1939–1946*. New Haven: Yale University Press.

Bangkok Post. 1990. 'Daichi reveals new plans for rebuilding Rangoon'. 19 April.

Bayly, Christopher and Tim Harper. 2004. *Forgotten Armies: the Fall of British Asia, 1941–1945*. London: Allen Lane.

Biruma Jōhō [Burma Information]. 1988. Tokyo: Nihon–Biruma Kyōkai, no. 375, November.

——. 1989. Tokyo: Nihon–Biruma Kyōkai, no. 379, March.

Brief History of the Myanmar Army. 1999. Rangoon: Defence Services Museum and Historical Research Institute.

Burma. 1944. Rangoon: Foreign Affairs Association, vol. 1, no. 1, September.

Burma Action Group. 1996. *Burma: the Alternative Guide*. London.

Burma Information Network – Japan. 2003. 'Is Japan really getting tough on Burma? (Not likely)', 28 June 2003.

Daily Report: East Asia. 1988. 'Japanese urged to stay away from Burma' (Kyodo, 10 August 1988). Foreign Broadcast Information Service, FBIS-EAS-88-155, 11 August, p. 6.

——. 1988a. 'Envoy advises residents to leave' (Kyodo, 8 September 1988). Foreign Broadcast Information Service, FBIS-EAS-88-174, 8 September, p. 3.

——. 1988b. 'Khin Nyunt meets with Military Attachés.' Foreign Broadcast Information Service, FBIS-EAS-88-185, 23 September, p. 21.

——. 1989. 'Foreign Ministry suspends grant aid to Burma' (Kyodo, 13

January 1989). Foreign Broadcast Information Service, FBIS-EAS-89-009, 13 January, p. 1.

——. 1989a. 'Thai daily on "foreign pressure" on regime' (Bangkok, *The Nation*, 6 January. Foreign Broadcast Information Service, FBIS-EAS-89-004, 6 January, pp. 36, 37.

——. 1989b. 'Government officially recognizes Burma (Kyodo, 18 February 1989). Foreign Broadcast Information Service, FBIS-EAS-89-032, 17 February 1989, p. 10.

——. 1989c. 'Thai paper interviews Aung San Suu Kyi' (Bangkok, *The Nation*, 23 February). Foreign Broadcast Information Service, FBIS-EAS-89-037, 27 February, pp. 39, 40.

——. 1989d. 'Burmese government recognition draws criticism' (Kyodo, 8 April). Foreign Broadcast Information Service, FBIS-EAS-89-067, 10 April, pp. 7, 8.

——. 1990. 'Saw Maung meeting detailed' (Kyodo, 30 August 1990). Foreign Broadcast Information Service, FBIS-EAS-90-172, 5 September, p. 45.

——. 1990a. 'Obstruction of Inquiry Noted' (AFP, Hong Kong, 7 November 1990). Foreign Broadcast Information Service, FBIS-EAS-90-216, 7 November, p. 28.

——. 1990b. 'Burmese placing hope in UN official's visit' (Bangkok, *The Nation*, 9 November 1990), Foreign Broadcast Information Service, FBIS-EAS-90-218, 9 November, p. 41.

Daily Yomiuri. 1996. 'Japan worried'. 23 May.

Daley, Matthew P. 2003. 'Testimony by Assistant Secretary Matthew P. Daley, Bureau of East Asian and Pacific Affairs, U.S. Department of State.' U.S. House of Representatives, Committee on International Relations, 2 October, at <wwwa.house.gov./ international relations>.

Dawn. 1990. 'Japanese investments'. All Burma Students' Democratic Front, January 1990, p. 13.

Earthrights International. 2000. *Total Denial Continues: Earth Rights Abuses along the Yadana and Yetagun Pipelines in Burma.* May, at www.earthrights.org/pubs/TotalDenialContinues.pdf.

Economist Intelligence Unit. 1996. *Country Report: Myanmar (Burma),* second quarter. London, E.I.U.

Facts about Burma. 1986. Rangoon, n.p.

Fairclough, Gordon. 1995. 'Lady in waiting'. *Far Eastern Economic Review*, 31 August, p. 26.

Far Eastern Economic Review. 1955. 'Survey of Burma'. 8 September, at www.feer.com.

——. 1960. 'Burma: Boycott on Japanese Goods'. 14 January, at www.feer.com.

——. 1991. 'Lack of rapport'. 4 July, p. 8.

——. 1994a. 'Daiwa's pledge'. 15 December, p. 65.

——. 1994b. 'Burma: Japanese resume aid'. 17 November, p. 13.

——. 1995. 'Burma bulls'. 23 March, p. 12.

Furnivall, John S. 1948. *Colonial Policy and Practice: A Comparative Study of Burma and Netherlands India.* Cambridge: Cambridge University Press.

Gaikō Foramu [*Diplomacy Forum*]. 1988. 'Enjo taikoku e no jōken' [Conditions for Japan to become an ODA Great Power], vol. 3, no. 12, December, pp. 22–37.

Government of Burma. 1943. *Burma During the Japanese Occupation.* Simla: Government of Burma, Intelligence Bureau.

Guyot, Dorothy H. 1966. *Political Impact of the Japanese Occupation of Burma* (Ph.D. Dissertation, Yale University). Ann Arbor: University Microfilms.

——. 2001. 'Myanmar and Indonesia: Inspirations for Japanese Novels and Memoirs since World War II'. In *Proceedings* of the Views and Visions Conference (18–20 December 2000). Rangoon: Universities Historical Research Centre, pp. 87–100.

Hadley, Paul. 1990. 'Unequal partners'. *Far Eastern Economic Review.* 3 May, pp. 51, 52.

Hall, D.G.E. 1960. *Burma.* 3rd ed. London: Hutchinson University Library.

Hasegawa Michiko. 1984. 'A Postwar View of the Greater East Asia War'. Translation of an article in the *Chūō Kōron*, April 1983. *Japan Echo*, 11 (special issue): pp. 29–37.

Hayashi Fusao. 2001. *Dai Tōa Sensō Kōtei Ron* [an Affirmation of the Greater East Asia War]. Tokyo: Natsume Shobō.

Hla Myint, Dr. 1997. 'The Role of the Health Sector Contributing to National Consolidation'. In *Socio-Economic Factors Contributing to National Consolidation*. Rangoon: Ministry of Defence, Office of Strategic Studies, pp. 97–106.

Holloway, Nigel. 1988. 'Japan to the rescue?' *Far Eastern Economic Review*, 25 August, pp. 10, 11.

——. 1989. 'Muted Harping'. *Far Eastern Economic Review*, 16 March, pp. 20, 21.

Houtman, Gustaaf. 1999. *Mental Culture in Burmese Crisis Politics: Aung San Suu Kyi and the National League for Democracy*. Tokyo: Tokyo University of Foreign Studies.

Inada Juichi. 1990. 'Ajia jōsei no hendō to Nihon no ODA [Changes in Asia and Japan's ODA]'. *Kokusai Mondai*, no. 360, March, pp. 45–59.

Institute of Developing Economies (IDE). 1983. *Basic Survey for Promotion of Official Loans to Burma*. Tokyo: IDE.

International Herald Tribune. 1996. 'Voices from Asia'. 6 February.

International Monetary Fund. 1990. *International Financial Statistics Yearbook, 1990*. Washington D.C.

The Irrawaddy. 1998. 'Japan seeks respect – but from whom?' Vol. 6, no. 2, 1998, at www.irrawaddy.org.

——. 1998a. 'All along the Watchtower', vol. 6, no. 5, September, at www.irrawaddy.org/database/1998/vol6.5/watcht

——. 2003. 'Rangoon blast kills at least one'. 27 March, on-line at www.irrawaddy.org.

——. 2004. 'Quotes of the month'. Vol. 12, no. 7, July, p. 3.

Ishigaki Shirō. 1988. 'Kinkyū kokusai rupo: gokuhi bunsho [urgent international report: top secret document]'. *Zaikai Tembō*, December, pp. 72–77.

Izumiya Tatsurō. 1985. *The Minami Kikan*. Transl. by U Aung Tun Chain. 2nd ed. Rangoon: Higher Education Department.

Japan International Cooperation Agency (JICA). 1988. *Gijutsu Kyōryoku Kokubetsu Shiryō: Biruma* [Country data on technical cooperation: Burma]. Series no. 79. Tokyo: JICA.

——. 2001. 'The Sound of joy: Japanese love buckwheat, but few know that Japanese aid is used to cultivate buckwheat in the former opium poppy fields of Myanmar'. *JICA Network*, at www.jica.go.jp.

Japan. Ministry of Foreign Affairs. 1987–1990. *Waga Kuni no Seifu Kaihatsu Enjo*, vol. 2, *Kokubetsu jisseki* [Japan's official development assistance; vol. 2, country data]. Tokyo: Association for Promotion of International Cooperation.

——. 1990. 'General election in Myanmar' (statement by Press secretary/ director- general for public affairs), Foreign Ministry, 2 July.

——. 1995. *Waga Kuni no Seifu Kaihatsu Enjo*, 2 vols., [Japan's official development assistance]. Tokyo, Association for Promotion of International Cooperation.

——. 1995a. 'Grant-in-aid to Myanmar for Project of Expansion of the Institute of Nursing', Foreign Press Centre-Japan, 30 October.

——. 2001–2004. *Seifu Kaihatsu Enjo (ODA): Kokubetsu Data Bukku* [Official development assistance: country data book]. Tokyo: Association for Promotion of International Cooperation.

Japan. Ministry of International Trade and Industry (MITI). 1958– 2000. *Keizai Kyōryoku no Genjō to Mondaiten* [the present state and problems of economic cooperation]. Tokyo: MITI.

Japan Network on Debt and Poverty. 2003. 'Japan Announces Debt Cancellation', 15 January, at www.jubilee2000uk.org/jmi/jmi-news/ japan150103.htm.

The Japan Times. 1992. 'Bridge touted as ODA success story'. 1 June.

——. 1994. 'Record tally in Diet wants Suu Kyi freed'. 2 April.

——. 1995. 'Yen 1 billion grant-in-aid to be extended to Myanmar'. 18 March.

——. 1995a. 'Myanmar opens dam built with Japanese assistance'. 2 May.

——. 1996. 'Arrests won't further curtail aid'. 24 May.

——. 2005. 'Japan gave 15 refugee status in '04'. 25 February.

'Japanese Grant for Repair of Baluchaung Hydropower Plant II: Questions and Responses between Lower House MP Nobuhiko Sutō and the Government of Japan.' 2001. (Unofficial translation, answers dated 29 June).

Jennings, Ralph. 2005. 'Mekong Basin Work Seen as Preparations: Aid Reveals Japan's Grand Designs for Asia'. *The Japan Times*, 8 July.

Johnson, Chalmers. 1962. *Peasant Nationalism and Communist Power: the Emergence of Revolutionary China, 1937–1945*. Stanford: Stanford University Press.

Kakazu Hiroshi. 1991. 'The Boomerang Economy and Prospects: the case of the Ryukyu Islands'. Paper presented at the International Society for Ryukyuan Studies, Symposium/Workshop, Naha, 9 August.

Keay, John. 2000. *India: A History*. New York: Atlantic Monthly Press.

Ko Jay. 2005. 'The disciplined road ahead'. *The Irrawaddy* on-line, March 28, at www.irrawaddy.org.

Kosai Yutaka and Matsuyama Kenji. 1991. 'Japanese Economic Cooperation'. *The Annals of the American Academy of Political and Social Science*, vol. 513, January, pp. 62–75.

Koshida Takashi. 1991. *Ajia no Kyōkasho ni kakareta Nihon no Sensō* [Japan's war as depicted in Asian textbooks]. Tokyo: Nashi no Ki Sha.

Kyodo News Service. 2002. 'Ban on trade by foreign firms'. 5 April.

Kudō Toshihiro. 1994. 'Japan's aid to Burma: Challenge to an Aid Power'. Unpublished paper, Cambridge University.

Kyaw Yin Hlaing. 2003. 'Reconsidering the failure of the Burma Socialist Programme Party government to eradicate internal economic impediments'. *Southeast Asia Research*, vol. 11: 1, March, pp. 5–58.

Lawrence, Neil. 2002. 'Japan's Hidden Refugees'. *The Irrawaddy*, vol. 8, no. 10, October.

Lintner, Bertil. 1988. 'Aung Gyi's anguish'. *Far Eastern Economic Review*, 28 July, p. 18.

——. 1989. *Outrage: Burma's Struggle for Democracy*. Hong Kong: Review Publications.

——. 1989a. 'Disciplined grief'. *Far Eastern Economic Review*, 12 January, p. 13.

——. 1991. 'One-way "Open door"'. *Far Eastern Economic Review*, 4 July: pp. 28, 29.

——. 1992. 'Hoshi uranai kan no kai: Myanmar to Nihon no tokushu kankei' [the mystery of the astrological hall: Myanmar and Japan's special relationship]. *AERA: Asahi Shimbun Weekly*, 30 June 1992, pp. 26–29.

——. 1995. 'Generals' gambit'. *Far Eastern Economic Review*, 20 July, pp. 14, 15.

——. 1999. *Burma in Revolt: Opium and Insurgency since 1948*. 2nd ed. Chiang Mai, Thailand: Silkworm Books.

——. 2001. 'Ray of hope'. *Far Eastern Economic Review*, 25 January, p. 22.

Mainichi Daily News. 1996. 'Business group upgrades ties with Burma'. 29 May.

——. 1996a. 'Japan hints at tough economic action if junta arrests Suu Kyi'. 20 June.

——. 1996b. 'Mainichi wins award for Burma column'. 5 September.

Mainichi Shimbun. 1991. 'Chief cabinet secretary Sakamoto urges "removal of house Arrest of Suu Kyi"'. 16 October, p. 3 [United States embassy, Tokyo, translation].

——. 1991a. 'Myanmā no "jinken" kyōgi [Discussion on 'human rights' in Myanmar]'. 25 December, p. 2.

Mainichi Shimbun Sha. 1990. *Kokusai Enjo Bijinesu* [the International Aid Business]. Tokyo: Aki Shobō.

Martin, Edward W. 1977. 'Burma in 1976: the beginnings of change?' *Asian Survey*, vol. 17: 2, February, pp. 155–159.

Masaki Hisane. 1995. 'Myanmar nurse school to get aid'. *The Japan Times*, 12 October.

——. 1995a. 'Japan–Myanmar relationship comes into focus'. *The Japan Times*, 27 October.

——. 1998. 'New envoy tells critics: yen loans for Myanmar fall within humanitarian bounds'. *The Japan Times*, 13 March.

Matthews, Bruce. 2001. 'Myanmar: Beyond the Reach of International Relief?' In *Southeast Asian Affairs 2001*. Singapore: Institute of Southeast Asian Studies, pp. 229–248.

Maung Maung, Dr. 1969. *Burma and General Ne Win*. Rangoon: Religious Affairs Department Press.

Maung Maung, U. 1989. *Burmese Nationalist Movements*. Edinburgh: Kiscadale.

'Maung Myanmar'. 1990. 'Open Letter to Japan Socialist Party leader Takako Doi for 177,000 Myanmar conscripted labourers'. *Working People's Daily*, 17–18 December.

McCrae, Alister. 1990. *Scots in Burma*. Edinburgh: Kiscadale.

Mekong Watch. 2001. 'Development, Environment and Human Rights in Burma/Myanmar: Examining the Impacts of ODA and Investment'. Tokyo: Public Symposium Report, December 15.

——. 2004. 'Topic: did Japanese ODA really stop after the Massacre on May 30th, 2003?' 27 May.

Mi Mi Khaing. ca 1950s. 'Kanbawza – A Modern Review'. Published in *The Nation*, Rangoon, and posted on the Online Burma Library at: www.burmalibrary.org.

Morrison, Ian. 1947. *Grandfather Longlegs: the Life and Gallant Death of Major H.P. Seagrim*. London: Faber and Faber.

Mya Maung. 1992. *Totalitarianism in Burma: Prospects for Economic Development*. New York: Paragon House.

Mya Than and Ananda Rajah. 1996. 'Urban Management in Myanmar: Yangon'. In Jurgen Ruland (ed.), *The Dynamics of Metropolitan Management in Southeast Asia*. Singapore: Institute of Southeast Asian Studies, pp. 225–252.

Myanmā Nyūsu [Myanmar News]. 1991. 'Nihon–Myanmā Kyōkai enkaku' [History of the Japan–Myanmar Association]. No. 404, May.

——. 1994. 'Keidanren mission no Myanmā hōmon [Visit of Keidanren mission to Myanmar]'. No. 438, July, pp. 11–20.

——. 1995–1996. 'Maung Aye SLORC fuku gichō no rai Nichi [SLORC vice chairman Maung Aye visits Japan]'. No. 454, December–January, pp. 4, 5.

Nagai Hiroshi. 1997. 'Yuganda media no naka no Biruma [Burma in the distorted Media]'. *Sekai*, no. 638, August, pp. 295–304.

Nemoto Kei. 1996. 'Aung San Suu Kyi: her Dream and Reality.' In Sugita Yoneyuki (ed.), *Aung San Suu Kyi and Contemporary Burma*. KIAPS Discussion Paper No. 1. Osaka: Kansai Institute of Asia–Pacific Studies, pp. 1–16.

Nihon–Biruma Kyōkai. 1989. *Yōbōsho* [Petition], 25 January.

Nihon Hōsō Kyōkai (NHK). 1990. Evening news, 10 November.

——. 1991. 'Dai Hon'ei Himitsu Shiryō: Biruma dokuritsu o enjo seyo [Secret files from the Imperial General Staff: assist Burmese Independence]'. 9 October.

Nihon Keizai Shimbun. 1991. 'Foreign minister Nakayama urges democratization efforts of Myanmar foreign minister'. 19 October, p. 2 [United States embassy, Tokyo, translation].

Nu, Thakin (U Nu). 1954. *Burma Under the Japanese.* New York: Macmillan and Company.

Ohmae Kenichi. 1997. 'Mrs. Suu Kyi is becoming a burden for a developing Myanmar' [English translation supplied by the Burma Relief Centre-Japan, 29 December]. *Sapio,* 12 November.

——. 1997a. 'Cheap and hardworking labourers: this country will be Asia's best' [English translation supplied by the Burma Relief Centre-Japan, 29 December]. *Sapio,* 26 November.

——. 1997b. '1997: a Year of Transition'. *Asiaweek.* December, pp. 5–8.

Olson, Lawrence. 1961. 'Japanese activities in Burma: Comments on Japan–Burma Economic Relations'. *Reports Service.* East Asia Series, vol. IX: 12 (Japan) New York: American University Field Staff, November 30.

Organization for Economic Development and Cooperation (OECD). 1969–2003. *Geographical Distribution of Financial Flows to Developing Countries.* Paris: Organization for Economic Development and Cooperation.

Orr, Robert. 1990. *The Emergence of Japan's Foreign Aid Power.* New York: Columbia University Press.

Pearn, B.R. 1939. *A History of Rangoon.* Rangoon: American Baptist Missionary Press.

Peiris, Denzil. 1974. 'Socialism without commitment'. *Far Eastern Economic Review.* 13 September, pp. 27–32.

People's Forum on Burma. 2004. 'Lawyers' Group for the Burmese Refugee Applicants in Japan'. 16 December, at <www1.jca.apc.org/pfb/menu.htm>.

Perlez, Jane. 2004. 'Across Asia, Beijing's Star is in Ascendance'. *The New York Times.* 28 August.

Pranee Tinakorn. 1990. 'Japan's Economic Assistance to Thailand'. In Yoshihara Kunio (ed.), *Japan in Thailand*. Kuala Lumpur: Falcon Press, pp. 51–76.

Price, John. 'A Just Peace? The 1951 San Francisco Peace Treaty in Historical Perspective'. Japan Policy Research Institute, JPRI *Working Paper* no. 78. June 2001 (www.jpri.org).

Reuters News Agency. 2001. 'US Objects to Japanese grant for Burma'. 15 May.

——. 2003. 'Japan dissatisfied with Myanmar Suu Kyi response'. 4 July.

Richburg, Keith B. 1989. 'Burma's military junta poses dilemma for foreign countries'. *The Washington Post*, 11 March, p. A20.

Rix, Allen. 1989–1990. 'Japan's Foreign Aid Policy: a Capacity for Leadership?' *Pacific Affairs*, vol. 62: 4, winter, pp. 461–75.

Rudner, Martin. 1989. 'Japanese official development assistance to Southeast Asia'. *Modern Asian Studies*, vol. 23: 1, pp. 73–116.

Ryūkyū Shimpō. 1996. 'Myanmā demise kasoku [Setting up branches in Myanmar accelerates]7. 4 August.

——. 1997. 'Yangon kūkō enjo miokuri [postponement of aid for Yangon airport]'. 31 August.

——. 2000. 'Jitto gaman no Nihon kigyō [Japanese firms enduring]'. 24 January.

Saitō Teruko. 1989. 'Tai Biruma ODA (seifu kaihatsu enjo): "enjo" ga maneita keizai, kankyō hametsu e no michi to Nihon no sekinin [Development assistance to Burma: the road to economic and environmental disaster caused by aid and Japan's responsibility]'. *Gendai Nōgyō*, November, pp. 58–67.

——. 1989a. 'Biruma gunsei ni yuchaku Nihon manē: Nihon O.D.A. wa Biruma ni tai shite donna yakuwari o hatashita ka? [Japanese money and the Burmese military regime: what role does Japanese O.D.A. play in Burma?]'. *Ajia no Tomo*, no. 8, August, pp. 4–10.

——. 1992. 'Japan's inconsistent approach to Burma'. *Japan Quarterly*, vol. 39: 1, January–March, pp. 17–27.

Saitō Teruko and Lee Kin Kiong. 1999. *Statistics on the Burmese Economy: the 19th and 20th Centuries*. Singapore: Institute of Southeast Asian Studies.

Sankei Shimbun. 2000. 'Yugo ga hoshū katagawari [Yugoslavia to bear the burden of repairs]'. 18 December, p. 1.

Sayre, Jerome. 1989. 'Burmese government recognition draws criticism'. Kyodo News Service, 8 April 1989 [in Foreign Broadcast Information Service, *Daily Report: East Asia*, FBIS-EAS-89-067, 10 April 1989].

Seekins, Donald M. 1992. 'Japan's Relations with Military Regimes in Burma: the *Kokunaika* Process'. *Asian Survey*, vol. 32, no. 2, pp. 246–262.

——. 1998. '"One Trip to Myanmar and Everyone would Love the Country': Japan Incorporated Rolls Out a Big Gun'. *Burma Debate*, vol. 5, no. 1, Winter, pp. 12–17.

——. 1999. 'The North Wind and the Sun: Japan's Response to the Political Crisis in Burma, 1988–1998'. *Journal of Burma Studies*, vol. 4, pp. 1–34.

——. 2000. 'Burma in 1999: a Slim Hope'. *Asian Survey*, vol. 40, no. 1 January– February, pp. 16–24.

——. 2002. 'Burma's Japanese Interlude, 1941–45: did Japan Liberate Burma?' Japan Policy Research Institute (JPRI) *Working Paper*, no. 87. August, 10 pp.

——. 2002a. 'From Myth to History: "Greater East Asia" (1941–1945) and Political Order in Southeast Asia'. Presented at the First Conference of the Swedish Association of Asia–Pacific Studies, University of Gothenburg, Sweden, 22 September 2002.

Selth, Andrew. 1989. 'Death of a Hero: the U Thant Disturbances in Burma, December 1974'. Griffith University *Australia–Asia Papers*, research paper no. 49, April.

Sender, Henny. 1996. 'The Sun never sets'. *Far Eastern Economic Review*. 1 February, pp. 46–48, 50.

Silverstein, Josef. 1982. 'Burma in 1981: the Changing of the Guardians begins'. *Asian Survey*, vol. 22: 2, February, pp. 180–190.

Smith, Martin. 1999. *Burma: Insurgency and the Politics of Ethnicity*. 2nd ed. London/Bangkok/Dhaka: Zed Books/White Lotus/The University Press.

Söderberg, Marie. 1996. *The Business of Japanese Foreign Aid: Five Case Studies from Asia*. London: Routledge.

Spiro, Melford E. 1982. *Buddhism and Society: a Great Tradition and Its Burmese Vicissitudes.* 2nd ed. Berkeley: University of California Press.

Steinberg, David I. 1990. 'Japanese economic assistance to Burma: Aid in the *"Tarenagashi"* Manner?' *Crossroads*, vol. 5: 2, pp. 51–107.

——. 1990a. *The Future of Burma: Crisis and Choice in Myanmar.* Lanham: University Press of America for the Asia Society.

——. 2001. *Burma: the State of Myanmar.* Washington DC: Georgetown University Press.

——. 2001a. 'Burma has done Nothing to Deserve Japan's Aid Reward'. *International Herald Tribune*, 28–29 April.

Suthy Prasartset. 1990. 'An Emerging Trade Pattern since the New Wave of Japan's Direct Investment in Thailand'. In Yoshihara Kunio (ed.), *Japan in Thailand.* Kuala Lumpur: Falcon Press, pp. 77–109.

Takeyama Michio. 1966. *Harp of Burma.* Trans. by Howard Hibbett. Tokyo: Charles E. Tuttle.

Tamayama Kazuo and John Nunneley. 2001. *Tales by Japanese Soldiers.* Cassell Military Paperbacks. London: Cassell and Co.

Tanabe Hisao. 1987. 'Japanese Ex-soldiers' view on Burma Appeared in their War Memoirs [*sic*]'. In the Burma Research Group, *Burma and Japan: Basic Studies on their Culture and Social Structure.* Tokyo: Tokyo University of Foreign Studies, pp. 308–312.

Tanabe Hisao and Utsumi Aiko. 1990. *Ajia kara mita 'Dai Tōa Kyōeiken'* [The 'Greater East Asia Co-Prosperity Sphere' seen from Asia]. Tokyo: Nashi no Ki Sha.

Thanmani, Bo. 1990. 'Criticism of atrocities of the old Japanese Army'. *Working People's Daily*, 5–6 November.

THIS IS Yomiuri. 1996. 'Aung San Suu Kyi to no taiwa: Biruma (Myanmā) wa hyaku ten man ten no jitten [Talk with Aung San Suu Kyi: Burma wins ten points out of one hundred]'. June, pp. 200–209.

Tokyo Broadcasting System (TBS). 1994. *Jōhō Tokushū*, 24 July.

Tōnan Ajia Yōran [Survey of Southeast Asia]. 1982. Tokyo: Tōnan Ajia Chōsa Kai.

Toriumi Iwao. 1998. 'Chairman Iwao Toriumi's Speech at the Opening Ceremony of The Second Japan–Myanmar Joint Economic Conference', Rangoon, 21 May.

Trager, Frank N. and William L. Scully. 1978. 'Burma in 1977: cautious changes and a careful watch'. *Asian Survey*, vol. 18: 2, February, pp. 142–152.

Union of Burma, Government of. 1960. *Is Trust Vindicated? The Chronicle of a Trust, Striving, and Triumph*. Rangoon: Director of Information, Government of the Union of Burma.

Wai Phyo Myint. 2004. 'Another 200 buses to go in service in Yangon'. *Myanmar Times and Business Weekly*, 5–11 July, at www.myanmar. com/myanmartimes.

Walinsky, Louis J. 1962. *Economic Development in Burma: 1951–1960*. New York: The Twentieth Century Fund.

Weller, Marc. 1993. *Democracy and Politics in Burma: A Collection of Documents*. Manerplaw, Burma: National Coalition Government of the Union of Burma.

Wickman, Stephen B. 1983. 'The Economy'. In Frederica M. Bunge (ed.), *Burma: A Country Study*. Area Handbook Series. Washington DC: The American University, pp. 133–180.

Wingfield, Tom. 2000. 'Myanmar: Political Stasis and a Precarious Economy'. In *Southeast Asian Affairs 2000*. Singapore: Institute of Southeast Asian Studies, pp. 203–218.

Working People's Daily. 1989. 'State Law and Order Restoration Council General Saw Maung receives Japanese Ambassador'. 18 February, p. 1.

——. 1990. Cartoon, 5 October.

——. 1991. 'General Saw Maung's Armed Forces Day Speech'. 28 March.

Yanagihara, Toru. 1993. 'Japan's Foreign Aid to Bangladesh: Challenging the Dependency Syndrome?' In Bruce M. Koppel and Robert M. Orr, Jr. (eds), *Japan's Foreign Aid: Power and Policy in a New Era*. Boulder: Westview, pp. 198–202.

Yano Tōru. 1991. 'Reflections on Suu Kyi's Nobel Peace Prize'. *Newsletter*, Center for Southeast Asian Studies, Kyoto University, special issue, 29 November, pp. 2, 3.

Yawnghwe, Chao-Tzang. 1995. 'Burma: the Depoliticization of the Political'. In Muthiah Aligappa (ed.), *Political Legitimacy in Southeast Asia: the Quest for Moral Authority*. Stanford: Stanford University Press, pp. 170–192.

Yomiuri Shimbun. 1992. 'Kambojia wahei sokushin de itchi [agreement on promoting peace in Cambodia]'. 6 January, p. 3.

Yoon, Won Z. 1973. *Japan's Scheme for the Liberation of Burma: the Role of the Minami Kikan and the 'Thirty Comrades'.* Papers in International Studies/Southeast Asia Series, no. 27. Athens: Ohio University Southeast Asia Program.

Zöllner, Hans-Bernd. 1994. 'Fritz Werner in Burma: a Study on the German–Burmese Relations after World War II'. In Uta Gartner and Jens Lorenz (eds), *Tradition and Modernity in Myanmar.* Berliner Asien-Afrika Studien. Berlin: Humbolt University, pp. 197–203.

INDEX

San Francisco, Treaty of [1951],
   55, 84 (note 2)
Sankei Shimbun on Baluchaung
   plant renovation, Chinese
   involvement, 143
Sasagawa Peace Foundation,
   142, 154
Seagrim, Hugh, 43, 44
self-government, colonial-era, 7
Shans, Shan States, vii, 9, 27
Smith Dun, Gen., 24
State Law and Order
   Restoration Council
   [SLORC]. *See* post-1988
   Military Regime
State Peace and Development
   Council [SPDC]. *See* post-
   1988 Military Regime
student activism, 6, 82
   in 1988, 88–90
Suzuki Keiji, Col., 17–22, 38
'Sweat Army', 13

tat [paramilitary units], 17
Tatmadaw [armed forces,
   Burmese], 4, 40, 41
   Japanese influence on, 22–24
   popular hatred of [1988], 90
   possibility of split in ranks,
   151
   young officers' plot [1976], 82
Thai–Burma Railway ('Railway
   of Death'), 13
Thakin Party [see Dobama
   Asiayone]

Than Shwe, Senior General
   [chairman of SPDC], 39
Thirty Comrades, 20–24
Trading companies, Japanese
   [*sōgō shōsha*], 76, 77, 116,
   118
Tun Tin, U, deputy prime
   minister, visits Japan
   [1988], 78, 79

United States policy on Burma,
   116, 145
   counter-productive nature of
   US sanctions, 152, 153

war narratives
   Burmese, 39–43
   Japanese, 44–51
   Karen, 43, 44
war reparations, Japan to
   Burma, 56, 57
   'Quasi-reparations', 57, 58
World War II in Burma,
   Japanese casualties, 13
   (text box), 44, 45
World War II in Burma,
   economic impact, 14
World War II in Burma,
   military operations, 13
   (text box)

Yadana project, Japanese
   participation in, 119, 122
Yōsei-shugi ['request-ism'], 72,
   73, 80, 83